NINE LEADERS IN ACTION

Proven Leadership Lessons
From Effective Leaders

CONTRIBUTING AUTHORS

Kris Safarova • Vincent Samat • Rishab Shah
Richmond Wong • Alice Qinhua Zhou • Aylwin Sim
Takahiro Ajimizu • Duddy Abdullah • Ismael Hernández

STRATEGYTRAINING.COM & FIRMSCONSULTING.COM

We increase the revenue and profits of consulting and professional services firms, and teach consulting skills to industry and government.

NINE LEADERS IN ACTION

We increase the revenue and profits of consulting and professional services firms, and teach consulting skills to industry and government.

A Kris Safarova | StrategyTraining.com & FIRMSconsulting.com Original
March 2022

Published & Printed in the United States of America by Firmsconsulting LLC.

www.firmsconsulting.com / www.strategytraining.com

Firmsconsulting business books are available at special discounts for bulk purchases for sales promotions or corporate use. Special editions, including personalized covers, excerpts of existing books, or books with corporate logos can be created in large quantities for special needs. For more information please contact **info@firmsconsulting.com**.

FIRMSCONSULTING L.L.C.
187 E. Warm Springs Rd.
Suite B158
Las Vegas, NV 89119
info@firmsconsulting.com

ISBN 978-1-956580-13-6

THIS BOOK IS DEDICATED TO OUR CLIENTS AROUND THE WORLD WHO WORK HARD TO SOLVE MANKIND'S TOUGHEST PROBLEMS.

CONTENTS

PREFACE

THE BOOK YOU ARE HOLDING IN YOUR HANDS is different from other leadership books.

First, you are not going to get perspectives on leadership from just one person. You are going to learn from nine different leaders who are succeeding against great odds. They can do so because of their ability to lead themselves and others as well as their perseverance and ability to demand the best of themselves.

Second, each chapter is written by a leader "in the trenches." Most leadership books are written by people who have been very successful, have since retired and are reflecting on their lives from a view of 9,000 feet, and piecing together a roadmap from their memories. That's helpful and can be very powerful, but there is unique value in getting wisdom and authentic experiences from leaders on the ground who are executing their career strategies in real time–those who are currently going through the leadership journey and are succeeding.

I handpicked eight of some of the most purpose driven, ambitious leaders I have ever met who are all "generals in active duty." As you read this book, know that they are busy implementing the advice you are reading.

All coauthors in this book are long-term clients of my company, FIRMSconsulting. I personally know each of them. Our mission is increase the revenue and profits of consulting firms, professional services firms, industry and government. You can find us at www.firmsconsulting.com and www.strategytraining.com.

Just recently we received an update from Andrew, whose entire journey is documented on our website through ~200 episodes. He thanked us for helping him build a consulting practice from zero revenue to approximately USD$30 million in recurring revenue over three years, and teaching him the sales programs and processes which he has since taken to the private sector to achieve results on an even larger scale. He is actively embedding a new sales process into his organization and transferring these skills across his team.

This is a testament of a great leader: someone who demands a lot of themselves and is willing to groom and develop others without being scared of strengthening competitors.

I live for those stories because this is why FIRMSconsulting was created and why we work tirelessly, including weekends, nights, and public holidays, so we can fulfill our mission to help clients around the world have a bigger impact.

I am starting with my chapter to set the right tone for this book. It will help you see that no matter the challenges you are facing right now, the boundaries of what is possible for you and what is possible in terms of your level of contribution to the world, are much bigger than you realize.

The biggest limits we have are the limits we have in our minds. If you don't believe something is possible, then you will most likely never achieve it. Not because you could not, but because you didn't believe you could.

And so, for me, the biggest objective I have for you from reading my chapter is to expand the boundary of what you believe is possible for you, your life, and your level of contribution.

Therefore, I recommend starting the book with Chapter 1 because it will help you understand why and how FIRMSconsulting was created, including my philosophy behind this book as well as the inspiration behind any of the work we do. Thereafter, you are welcome to read the rest of the chapters in any order you want. It is a choose-your-own-adventure type of book where every chapter has incredible value.

I hope you enjoy the book, and if you find it helpful, I will be grateful if you support the book with a review. If you would like sample episodes of the advanced training we use to help consulting firms, professional services firms, industry and government, please visit www.firmsconsulting.com/promo and submit your details.

Why not have a big life?

KRIS SAFAROVA
Founder & CEO
FIRMSconsulting.com & StrategyTraining.com
Wall Street Journal, USA *Today*, and *Amazon* Best Selling Author

CHAPTER 1

Cultivating Leadership With Determination

BY KRIS SAFAROVA

CLIENTS OFTEN SEE a summary of my life spread over three continents, from master classical concert pianist and management consultant to corporate banker and, today, the owner and CEO of a content-based media organization spanning top-ranked podcast channels, the world's largest strategy video streaming service, a book publisher and more. They want to know how I built a successful career and how I became an influential and impactful leader. It did not start this way, and I have found the best lessons come, not from my successes, but from mining the chokeholds in my life for the patterns that gave me the resiliency to persevere.

I have been told by many of my mentees and clients that the principles distilled from my life experiences have helped them remove mental blocks and become more impactful leaders, by giving them insights, greater confidence, hope, and tested approaches. Therefore, I am going to share some of them with you.

When I was five years old, my grandfather's payday always made for a long night in the dark streets of Samara, Russia.

My mother's father, Alexander, was employed as a factory worker at the time. It was far from his career of choice; he had always had a talent and passion for painting. He could recreate any painting. Because of his undeniable talent, he was offered a chance to attend an esteemed academy in St. Petersburg. The opportunity was a dream come true: It would be his first time studying painting in an academic capacity and to refine and develop the skill that he had honed all of his life.

Alexander's father shared no such sentiments. In the wake of the Russian Revolution, my ancestors were stripped of our possessions and assets such as a chocolate factory and a ship, Trofimov, that sailed the Volga River. What business, my grandfathers' father wondered, did a man have with painting—especially when the family was in such dire need of reliable labor and wages?

This is how Alexander became a factory worker, quashing his artistic aspirations to dust in the process. With his dreams eclipsed, he turned to the bottle. Alcoholism seized him greedily, and he lost track of all else in life—his wife and children included. Every day was the same mindless work—except for that precious time, once every month, when he was paid.

The money always went to the same place. Every month, dependable as clockwork, he bought all the liquor he could consume and drank himself to unconsciousness on the streets. His senseless body was an easy target for thieves and pickpockets: within hours he would be bare of any remaining money and would often be missing expensive articles of clothing, such as a hat or shoes.

So it was that month after month, his wife Galina, my grandmother, would take to the dark streets of Samara, scouring them for the prone form of her intoxicated husband. Accompanying her on some of these searches was their granddaughter: me. I was far too small to assist in carrying Alexander home; my earliest memories of this are from the age of three. Galina wouldn't allow me to exhaust myself with such a task–and I can promise you, I tried repeatedly. I was very persistent then, just as I am now. Instead, I would trail behind them, keeping a hold of Galina's handbag and making sure that my grandfather's limp feet didn't get stuck anywhere along the road.

I eventually left these endless, frigid nights far behind me, but I am never free of them. To this day, I'm haunted by thoughts of what could have been if Alexander had made the decision to stand up to his father. What if he had, after all, pursued painting? Would he have had a wife who never spoke to him except to argue? Would he have spent his nights and days in a minuscule closet that served as his excuse for a bedroom? Would he have had a granddaughter who, once a month, would trudge through Samara's windy streets, with one hand tightly holding a handbag that didn't belong to her and another trying to ensure that her grandfather's feet wouldn't be hurt?

I can't even begin to imagine the lives that my mother and grandmother could have led if my grandfather chose to pursue his dream. He was so incredibly talented and handsome. I think if he would have gone against his father's wishes and pursued painting, he would have had a meaningful life of contribution and massive professional accomplishments. I think this very event instilled in me a strong belief that you must follow your own voice. If you believe pursuing certain goals and dreams is right for your life, it's important not to let anyone convince you otherwise. Then, if you fail, you will at least know you did everything you could.

This is just one experience in my life that has helped to sculpt me into the leader that I am today. It helped me expand the boundaries of what I thought was possible for my life and not let anyone stop me in pursuing much bigger goals than what people around me thought were possible to accomplish.

Everyone is the product of their circumstances, and each of us has all sorts of lessons to be garnered from the places we've been, people we've known, and hardships we've endured. None of us lead easy lives, but that doesn't need to be a bad thing. Hard times make strong people, and strong people make good times, and good times make weak people. So, if you have faced a lot of hardships in your life, while it's a liability in terms of how it likely impacted your health and limitations it may have created in your mind, it's also an asset in terms of helping to shape you into a strong leader. Through our struggles, we become stronger individuals with more empathy, greater ambition, capability, and potential for great leadership.

Throughout this chapter, I invite you to accompany me through the major milestones within my life, hile also taking the time to consider your own. Though our experiences are likely to be drastically different, it is my hope that my journey will inspire and assist yours by sharing with you many of the core lessons and insights that allowed me to go far beyond what that three-year-old girl ever thought was possible.

TAKING LIFE BY THE REINS

My grandmother, Galina, could scarcely have been more different from her husband. To me, she seemed like a guardian angel—always coming to Alexander's rescue, supplying the funds for them both to keep scraping by, and—despite it all—still finding time to spend with me whilst my parents were preoccupied with my younger twin brothers. The two of us shared a fondness for bananas and ice cream, which we would only get to enjoy in late spring, when we could make a handful of spare change by selling lilacs from our backyard at the bus stop. After a few hours of selling, we would make enough kopeks to buy one banana or one ice cream for both of us.

Cancer was what took Galina in the end. Once her illness became terminal, she insisted that I never visit her. I will never know the exact reasons why. But my guess is, as much as it pained her not to see her granddaughter, she knew that her horribly sick appearance would be scarring, and she hoped to spare me from having to witness such pain.

At this point, I was an inquisitive preteen, in the midst of pursuing a music education, an artistic journey that my grandfather never got to experience. Though I loved her with all my heart, I refused to obey Galina's request. I collected coins from the street and sneaked onto public buses without paying to save money to buy her a gift.

It took a few weeks, but I managed to accumulate enough money to purchase one of each of my grandmother's favorite treats: one banana and one ice cream sandwich, the same things that we had enjoyed together on so many spring evenings at the bus stop after selling enough flowers to pay for them. By this time she did not have any teeth, not even one, so those were among the few types of food she could eat. I remember waiting for the time that I would grow up, so that I could feed my grandmother bananas every day. Even in my tiny little head, I knew it wouldn't be healthy for her to get by on ice cream alone.

I insisted that my grandmother eat the treats I had brought her. She initially wanted me to eat them instead, but I refused. Though she was glad to receive the treats, she made me promise her that I wouldn't come back until she asked for me. I knew that if you promise something, it can't be broken; yet, as reluctant as I felt, I still made the promise. As a consequence, I would only see her once more before she died.

I learned a valuable lesson the hard way through this experience: Be careful with the promises that you make. When you make a promise, you're committed to upholding it no matter what. A leader needs to be trustworthy, but they also need to avoid inhibitive commitments to operate freely. A promise is something of immense value, and it should be treated as such. I believed that in my childhood, as well as now, and therefore, I wasn't able to be there for my grandmother during her final moments. I lost far too much time that we could have had together. If I had been more cautious with the promises that I made in the first place, I could have been there as much as possible during the last chapter of her life, making it brighter, easier, less painful, and less lonely. And, quite frankly, this was one promise that, now looking back, I know should have been broken.

My grandfather, despite all the years of bitterness between them, was heartbroken by his wife's death. A year later, he exchanged his own last words with me: a bid goodnight, and a promise to stop drinking. That was a promise which he kept, but not in the way that he had intended: He would never get up from his bed again.

Despite the differences between them, my grandparents both taught me valuable lessons, without which, I would never have been the person I am today. Seeing each of them pass away after living a life of quiet desperation, I knew one thing for certain: I am responsible for my people. If I had been older to care for them, I could have shielded both of them from so much pain, and they could have had much bigger lives. And I knew I had that responsibility going forward for my siblings, for my parents, for my clients, for my friends, for my partner, and some day, God willing, for my own children.

Taking responsibility for your loved ones, for your team, for how you can help your clients in the most impactful way, is what makes you a great leader because your intention is to lookout for their best interest. People want to be led, but they only want to be led by someone who has their best interests at heart.

And, of course, I could not take responsibility for anyone before taking responsibility for my own life. I knew then that I would not fold to others' wishes if it would be detrimental for the bigger future, and I would never abandon my determination to achieve the biggest vision I could paint for my life and my level of contribution.

People should always do what is right for themselves as individuals, even when it goes against the wishes and opinions of others, so long as they don't hurt anyone in the process. My grandfather had incredible creative potential, but he allowed his family's wishes and their boundaries of what they thought was possible for my grandfather's level of achievement and contribution, to quash his aspirations. If he had taken his chance to pursue a career in painting, his life would have gone in a very different direction and so would that of his family. He was given this incredible talent that could have delighted millions of people, but instead, he lived a life of quiet desperation with the only highlight being drinking himself to an unconscious level once a month.

We are in control of our lives, and we should never let it go to waste. Yes, the cards we are given may not be the best, but we need to play the cards we are dealt. To be a leader to others, you first need to lead yourself. And, in leading yourself, you must aim to serve as an example, not a warning.

EMBRACING CHALLENGES

For as long as I can remember, people have treated me and my family differently. My father is from Azerbaijan, and he married my Russian mother. My parents worked harder than anyone I knew, but we nonetheless struggled with poverty and persistent discrimination. When I was just three years old, we were suddenly evicted from our rented apartment and given just a few hours to move out. I remember later that day walking through knee-deep snow on foot, in the darkness of the night. It was so hard to lift my tiny legs to make each next step. I remember not knowing if I could lift my little leg one more time, but each time I found the strength to do it. I didn't begrudge my parents; I understood that there was no room for me on the sledge, which carried our possessions as well as my newborn twin brothers. Putting me on the sledge would have resulted in them leaving behind some of our belongings. It's all too easy to recall the cold and the exhaustion that weighed down my every step, yet I knew that I could not give up. I still remember that walk as if it was yesterday: white snow, freezing cold, my cheeks and nose getting numb, and lifting one leg at a time. No. Matter. What.

I shoved down the pain, gritted my teeth, and pressed forward. This determination to press forward, no matter what, served me well as a leader. It allows you to lead yourself toward goals that are outside of your orbit of possibilities and eventually break out of your current orbit. And it allows you to be seen by your team as someone who they can rely on and believe in because they consistently see you pressing on in situations where most of the people they know would give up or just decide it is too hard and not worth the sacrifice.

Another important lesson from this story is that the risks are dependent not only on the confidence level one has but also on your level of resourcefulness and the level of resourcefulness of your team. My parents' plan worked because I, as a three-year-old, was resourceful to not give up and kept lifting my legs high enough to make every step required to finish that journey. So, as we select team members for our team, we need to find people who will be resourceful enough to not give up at crucial times.

It's important to not only focus on resources at your disposal when confronted with a challenge. Your ability to respond is not directly proportional to the sum of your resources. The greater the resources one has before starting, does not mean greater odds of success. I have seen many talented clients limited by a resources-based view of life who gave up on potentially lucrative opportunities because they wanted the comfort of having enough resources in place before pursuing those opportunities.

Resourcefulness, in contrast, is a belief that you will eventually figure things out; that you are able to assemble the resources needed or find a creative way to move forward with fewer resources. Resourceful leaders proceed before waiting for the resources to show up. As a leader of any organization, you know that resources are always limited, and demands are always unlimited. You trust yourself to learn, prioritize well, adjust, and build allies as you proceed. Your raison d'être, your 'why' as such, is so strong and meaningful to you that you know you will find a way to overcome the challenge.

In my own life, I've had to be resourceful because I had practically no resources starting out. Going back to my story, we eventually found a place to stay with several of my parents' friends. Couch surfing is much easier to arrange for one person than it is for a party of five; still, it was a roof over our heads, and it was enough to survive—barely. I remember watching my mother through a crack in the bedroom door as she asked whether we could spend just one more night. The answer was a firm, "Nyet," which in Russian means 'No.'

As I grew older, the situation in the former Soviet Union deteriorated sharply. I would watch as hungry, shivering families waited in line outside of grocery shops for hours, hoping that they would be able to purchase just one item before the shelves were once again laid bare. In times of such desperation, most people in Russia suffered. The nearly limitless potential of each and every individual was eclipsed, reduced to hunger and frailty. *Mavis*, a book of which I am the proudest, drew heavily from my experiences living through the collapse of the former Soviet Union.

I knew it was wrong. And I knew that when I grew up, I was not going to let myself, or anyone I could help, become nothing but another poverty data point.

At the time, my ambitions manifested through the pursuit of music; the artistic education that my grandfather had been forced to reject so many years ago. I had first applied when I was a child and was initially turned down; my mother, however, was having none of it. She wanted me to play the piano, and she wasn't willing to take no for an answer. She convinced the teachers to accept me out of sheer stubbornness, something that I would never forget.

Insistence and dedication, as my mother inadvertently taught me, can get you just about anywhere in life. 'No' doesn't mean 'never,' and a simple refusal to give up can be the most powerful tool of all. If you keep pressing forth, and if you can conjure innovative methods of working around the obstacles that you face, apparent impossibilities can become attainable.

Of course, such stolid determination wasn't always easy to maintain. As my education progressed, I encountered one hurdle after another. Even my daily commute to and from school could be a challenge, since

I had to navigate the bus system myself, my parents being occupied with my three younger siblings. I got lost more than once, and by the time that I was given the chance to perform internationally as an official music ambassador of the Russian Federation, resourcefulness was second nature to me. I traversed foreign countries—Germany, France, the Czech Republic, Bulgaria—excited to learn.

I knew then that I was going to seize opportunities the world had to offer—but it wasn't going to be easy.

Eventually, I was able to turn my music into a profession, though it wasn't a very lucrative one. I made the equivalent of less than three dollars per day—and that was when people bothered to pay me. I couldn't afford a taxi home, and that landed me in several dangerous situations. I was pursued, abducted, and assaulted on several occasions; curses and slurs were regularly spouted on the streets from men whose intentions I was afraid to even imagine.

One particular incident was especially scarring: My attackers had forced me at knifepoint to remove a ring gifted to me by my mother. They were about to cut off my finger to get it off but I managed to wrench the ring off with my teeth, taking no small amount of skin with it. The police weren't interested in my case, nor was the doctor at the hospital that I visited. Both, it seemed, had bigger things to worry about. The doctor left me with a particularly harsh message: Unless my attackers went so far as to slam my head into the street, I would be better advised not to waste his time.

This was my first visit to the hospital after a few years earlier. That time, my condition hadn't been so dismissible.

I was sixteen years old, and the victim of an allergic reaction so horrendous that I was deemed unlikely to ever recover. I was told that I could expect to live a month at the very most. It was, the doctors explained, the side effect of an untested vaccine—something that was and still is all too common in developing countries. They told me without much remorse that there was nothing they could do, and they didn't expect me to survive until the next day.

There's nothing quite like being looked in the eye and told that you had little chance of living to see the sunrise.

I survived the night, and the next night after that. Days grew into weeks, and eventually—despite constant insistence to the contrary—the swelling ruptured and went down. I was released from the hospital scared and scarred but intact, convinced now more than ever how brief our time was on this earth, and that I had to shape my own life versus letting society determine what is possible and not possible for me. I still have the scar on my face.

The brink of death puts everything into perspective. When you don't know whether you'll last another day, you realize just how long a single day is—and how much you can accomplish within it. My own brush with mortality taught me a crucial lesson: Any day, for reasons entirely outside of our control, everything can end. This may seem disheartening, but I view it in the opposite light. Knowing that my time is limited, I've made it my duty to push the boundaries while I still have time. Nothing could be worse than reaching the end of your life and realizing that days, months, or years of it were ultimately wasted: that you led an unlived life.

Something had to change. I first tried moving to Moscow. Even with the help of a family friend who worked in real estate, my living situation there was dire. The apartment where I lived was in such an awful condition that it couldn't possibly be rented to a paying tenant. Just about the only piece of furniture in the whole place was an ancient couch, choked with grime and infested with bedbugs. It had no bathtub, no shower, and no refrigerator. The plumbing was severely clogged, and the only way to heat water for bathing was with fire or electric kettle. In all, it was barely a step up from homelessness.

Yet, it became my home. I can't say I grew fond of it over time. Much to the contrary, I recall that period in Moscow as one of the most difficult times of my life. Though I had initially moved there in the hopes of finding a wider variety of professional opportunities, the opposite turned out to be true. To be employed in Moscow, I needed a special residency permit as well as a 'propiska'—a legal document stating that I owned either an apartment or a house. Purchasing a place to live, of course, was completely out of the question until I could make more money, much more money—but I couldn't make more money unless I could work.

Moscow, it turned out, was a dead end. I returned to Samara, but not for long; at this point, I knew that my only option was to leave Russia entirely.

The process of moving was a difficult one, both financially and emotionally. I was leaving my entire family behind and didn't know when I would get the opportunity to return. Unlike me, they had no interest in leaving Russia. On top of that, it was impossible for me to procure a visa to most developed countries without a sponsor. I finally managed to obtain a three-month visitor's visa to South Africa, and I jumped on the opportunity.

The next leg of my life began in a minuscule, cockroach-infested room in Johannesburg, with only $1,000 to my name. Did you know African cockroaches have wings and fly right at you when you surprise them?

It felt amazing to know that I was finally taking the necessary steps toward building a truly meaningful life. Being able to maintain gratitude for my circumstances, even when they were far from ideal, was one of the most powerful lessons that I've learned. When you focus on appreciation for what you have rather than expectations of what you want, you strengthen yourself on a profound level. Remembering that every struggle, or apparent failure, is just another step on the uneven road to success; building upon your existing assets will almost always serve to your betterment in the long run.

If not for my determination, you wouldn't be reading these words today; my disadvantages initially seemed insurmountable. Western life was entirely foreign to me, and my English skills had a long way to go. It seemed as though my music diploma wasn't going to help when it came to getting any reliable employment. The music college I graduated from wasn't even in a Western database, and I was therefore unable to get my diploma accredited. The job search itself wasn't easy. At one point, a would-be interview ended with me locked in the back of a gas station. It seemed, for quite a while, that life would never stop testing me.

But all things come to an end, even suffering. I was eventually hired as a front desk receptionist at a tiny company. My employer was a manufacturing company with very powerful clients, including senior leaders of the National Police and Armed Forces worldwide. From day one, I resolved to go above and beyond.

I am not sure where this came from, but in any job I had, I would always approach it as if I was the owner. I would care about everything related to the company, not just my areas of responsibility. I would do any work that I saw had to be done. I would constantly look for opportunities to reduce the costs and increase revenue. And that quality helped me tremendously in life. It helped me get noticed and be promoted in a significantly accelerated manner.

As a business leader myself, I know that any business leader would generally want people on their team that add bigger value than what it costs to have them on the team. Moreover, people rarely say no to free help, and once you start adding value above what is expected, you gain trust and are given more opportunities to add value. From there, you can identify the areas in which you can deliver unique value. If you can show people in senior roles how good you are, you're well on your way to being much more than a volunteer.

So, I fully dedicated myself to any valuable task I could find on top of my daily responsibilities. Physical labor, design work, negotiations, partnerships–nothing was off the table. I literally carried parcels and delivered mail by foot on the streets of Johannesburg. I worked long hours after clocking out for my day job, not for any money, but because I truly cared about the business and believed that it deserved my best efforts. As I continued to add more value, I was given more and more important responsibilities. I quickly rose in rank and landed a much larger position within the year.

None of this was easy. My initial salary was $500 a month and on many of the days, I did not have any money to buy lunch or dinner. I know that I wouldn't have been able to work so hard if not for my firm, unrelenting belief in my ability to figure things out. I feel the belief that you can figure things out is crucial to be a great leader when it comes to leading yourself and leading others.

At the same time, I knew that work experience alone wouldn't be enough to propel me into the higher branches of the business world. The truth, I had to admit to myself, was that I would need a recognized degree–one that could be found in the database, unlike my music diploma. I was still working with the manufacturing company when I began studying at the University of South Africa. At the university, I once more found myself struggling. I had to translate almost every word in any book or assignment which significantly slowed down my ability to work through the material. Whenever I sat down to study, I would make sure to have a dictionary on hand. Internet access was still very expensive for me then, so a paper dictionary was what allowed me to survive and excel as a student. Hours of time were spent at each study session just jotting translations above words in my textbooks. Only once I finished all that translation work was I able to get started on understanding the material for that study session and completing the assignments. I did all of this in addition to juggling my various jobs—the manufacturing company on the weekdays, teaching piano, teaching singing, teaching Russian, and working as a Russian translator on the weekends. I needed all these jobs to pay my bills.

My life was absolutely exhausting, but it was worthwhile. There was hope for a bigger life. When it came time to write the first set of exams, I was really scared I would fail. Not only did I pass, I got straight A's and was among the very top of my class. I am not sure how it was even possible given that my knowledge of the English language was so basic. At the end of every exam, I wrote: "Please forgive my mistakes. English is not my first language." Maybe that helped, and my teachers judged my performance based on my knowledge and not based on my grammar mistakes.

Though this period in my life was one of the most difficult, it was also one of the most valuable. It taught me the power of not giving up. It took me eight months of applying to any job I could find, and was qualified for, before I got the first $500 / month job.

It would have been easy to give up and just decide to focus 100% of my time on building my teaching and translation practice. My students were referring me and the site I managed to code was getting traction by getting me more clients, but I knew to achieve my bigger vision, I needed to spend time in the corporate world and get a recognized degree. This determination to press on despite how many times I heard 'No,' played a deciding role in finally landing that first job for $500 a month; the amount that barely covered rental cost and left no funds to buy food or to cover any other expenses. I could have earned more working as a teacher full-time, but that path was not aligned with my bigger vision. As a leader, you need to know where you are taking your team, even if the entire team is just you, for now. And by knowing where you are taking your team, you will then know the steps needed; some steps may look like a step back, but it is necessary to get to where you want to go.

SEIZING OPPORTUNITIES

At this point, many people in my position would have considered my music diploma, and career as a master classical concert pianist, to be nothing more than a signifier of an absurd waste of time. Yes, it had provided me with an opportunity to earn money for basic things like food, but what good was it possibly going to do for me in the long run?

As it turned out, it made all the difference in the world.

One night, I happened to find myself in attendance at a dinner involving several international companies meeting prospective high performing students, seated beside the local managing partner of a major consulting firm. As we conversed, I mentioned my music background, to which he responded with surprising interest. He, like all the best consultants, understood that the capacity for dedication and hard work are infinitely more valuable than anything one can glean from a textbook. When he learned that I hoped to enter a career in strategy consulting, he offered to meet with me to further explore my opportunities.

Yet, the process wasn't an easy one. After my meeting with the local managing director of a major consulting firm where he offered me a full-time role in a research department (since I did not have a recognized degree yet), I continued to contact the recruiter. No matter how many times I called, they failed to return my calls. Finally—perhaps just because they were fed up with me and my stubbornness—I was offered a temporary part-time position, entirely unlike the one that the managing director and I agreed on. Trying to get anything better, I was told, would be a losing battle. There was just no getting around the fact that I was too old and too underqualified.

I reached out to the managing director to politely refuse. I remained dignified despite my fear that I was missing out on potentially my only chance in life. I thanked him for the opportunity but mentioned I had bills to pay and could not accept a part-time role when I already had a full-time role.

The managing director was angry with the recruiter's behavior, and an offer for the initially agreed on position was made by the recruiter almost immediately thereafter. Though still extremely junior, it was full-time and permanent. That was my big break moment.

That position had virtually nothing to do with consulting itself. It also didn't offer any real opportunities for rank advancement. Per the job description, it wouldn't do much of anything to help me become an exceptional management consultant—and yet I seized the opportunity without a second thought. By that time in my life, I knew quite well that I had to take every chance that was presented to me.

From the moment I joined, I started looking for more opportunities within the firm. My experience at my previous job had taught me that the best way to advance is to go above and beyond, truly care about the organization as if it was my own business and make senior people's life as easy as I could. I focused on what I could contribute, making use of my unique talents to add above average value. In my experience, when you seek to make others' lives easier and better through your own contributions, senior people will want you on their teams. This is crucial to the build of a good leader. People don't follow leaders out of obligation or intimidation. To be truly committed, they must believe that you have their best interests at heart. Deeply caring about the well-being of the organization and your team will earn the trust of key people within the organization, while also shaping you into a person of whom you can be proud.

Importantly, this doesn't just apply to your current circumstances. If you build a strong foundation of trust within a certain company only to leave it in the dust at the first opportunity, you're doing more harm than if you had never forged those relationships in the first place. It's all about genuine loyalty, integrity, and being someone people can count on. Whenever I left a job, I always worked to make the transition as easy as possible for my current employer, often at great expense to myself. I would stay longer if they needed it and gladly finished up any extra work given to me, even once I was no longer on the payroll. A good relationship, whether it be personal or business-related, means caring about people even when you no longer need anything from them. In the same way, if you want to see if someone is a good fit for your organization—be it as a client, an employee, or a partner—or even to see if someone is a good fit to be your spouse or a friend, find ways to see how they will behave if they think they no longer want or need anything from you.

Soon enough, my attempts to go above and beyond opened a new opportunity: I found a partner whose work could benefit from my unique abilities. He was working on a market entry case, specifically pertaining to the Eastern European market—something to which I, because of my upbringing, could make a valuable contribution. I asked him whether I could help with the project, saying that I would work as a volunteer, outside of my normal hours. With an offer that good, I figured it would be just about impossible to turn me down—and he agreed.

As always, I gave the project my full effort and complete attention. I still made sure to perform well in my research role, but from the time my regular work ended, I switched gears to the consulting project. I worked tirelessly, picking up the slack when others fell behind, and ultimately ended up being rewarded for my efforts with a promotion: My work was so valuable to the partner, that I was able to become a full-time business analyst on his team. I continued to rise in rank, and within a handful of months, I became a superior to the analysts who had refused to even talk to me when I was in my research position. I was at the level of MBA graduates and on a career track to the partnership.

My strategy those days was simple and has never failed me. One hundred percent of my attention was dedicated to my work. This left little room for socializing, but I didn't mind. I knew what I wanted, and I knew how to get it. Any free time was devoted to studying, and I kept my sleep to the minimum number of hours necessary to maintain my efficiency.

Some people like to say that hard work is its own reward. I don't think that's exactly accurate. Hard work is just that: *hard*. It can be exhausting, grueling, and dull. But it will almost always earn you something. If you're truly motivated, not just by the possibility for your success but by the level of contribution that you can reach—and if you can use that motivation as fuel—you'll quite possibly find yourself reaching heights that you never could have imagined.

At age 26, that was exactly where I found myself. I graduated all of my classes with distinction, *cum laude*, and I'd had the opportunity through my work to meet with several internationally significant figures, including the former finance minister of Russia, a crown jewel client, and heads of major organizations around the world. I even began to build a relationship with a billionaire client–a man whose many accomplishments included a close relationship with the late former President Nelson Mandela. Despite all adversity, I was making gigantic strides in my business career. I was promoted once again, effectively being promoted three times where some people who joined at the time when I joined, had not been promoted even once. More than that, I was finally making a real difference in the world, and I no longer had to count coins to see if I could buy lunch that day.

One of the key qualities that made me a good leader during this period continued to be my ability to take responsibility for broader projects. That allowed me to lead not only my team but also even a client in certain situations where that was necessary. There was one situation where a project was in a lot of trouble. There was only about one week left before the presentation to the board, and the team failed to make sufficient progress. I was called to come in and save the project because of the reputation I had built to be a type of person who takes responsibility well beyond my allotted portion and who can accomplish what an average senior consultant (my position at the time) couldn't.

I remember during that project that the client was based in one of the buildings in the same office park where our consulting offices were located. I arrived that morning to find out that something went terribly wrong: The team had nothing to show for weeks of work, and the board meeting was fast approaching. The client was very concerned about his career but he felt it was his fault as well that the project got off the rails. He mentioned to me that he knew it was not possible to deliver the entire business case by the deadline, but maybe I could help with putting together one or two sections.

But that is not how my mind works. I would be working, till the last second if I had to, in the hope to finish what was needed to over-deliver at that board meeting. I was not coming there to get 10% of the work done. So, even though I was not the most senior person in that team, and certainly was less senior than the client, I took leadership of the project; we worked hard, and we delivered the full business case on time. That client was a crown jewel client, and he sent an email to the senior partners in the consulting firm mentioning my role in saving the project. This story would have never happened if I did not have that quality of taking responsibility. I truly believe it makes you a very effective and influential leader. I highly recommend you adopt that approach to viewing things for your own leadership journey.

Here, as well as during many other parts of my life, I experienced the power of momentum. When things start to play out in your favor, you need to capitalize on that positive momentum to make the most out of it. This doesn't just apply to your career and business, but to all areas of your life: contribution efforts, social, romantic, familial, and so on. On the other hand, when negative momentum begins to build, you need to work as hard as you can to convert it into something positive. Whenever I see someone get a job at a new company, I recommend that they apply their maximum effort during their first 90 days. It's during these days that your reputation as a leader, as a contributor, whether you are "executive material", is established, and once you've shown yourself to be a certain type of person in the eyes of coworkers, customers, and clients, it can be very hard to alter that image.

A good leader is always on the lookout for chances to improve themselves and their team. If you expect opportunities to be handed to you, you'll never be able to make genuine progress in your life and your career. Success comes from active effort. When you see a chance for adding value well beyond what is expected of you, and that contribution is aligned with your purpose in life, don't let it slip away. Rebuilding that momentum can be very difficult.

FACING ADVERSITY

Throughout my professional and personal life, I've come to learn that adversity is one of the greatest sources of strength. It's how you manage adversity that will determine success or failure. Whenever I find myself staring down a challenge, I remind myself of how much I've already overcome, and I remember that almost no obstacle is truly insurmountable.

Still, there are times when it's easy to feel overwhelmed, especially when the adversity itself is never-ending. No matter how many times I prove myself and my capabilities, some people still disdain and discredit me for the fact that I am a woman in business and that I speak with an accent. They will never mention this as the reason to dismiss me and my ideas, but they often celebrate the very same idea I had had, when it is repeated by a male colleague. This is a common occurrence even today. Someone once negatively mentioned my gender five to six times in one of my book reviews, and that review was upvoted 42 times. This seemed to be the most important issue for the reviewer. This just shows that many people still discriminate against females, especially when they can do so behind the cover of anonymity.

One day, following a successful presentation during which I helped persuade the board of directors to continue working with my firm, I was sitting in the car with two male partners of the firm. One of them commented on my great work, saying that I was a "valuable asset" to the company. The other replied with a muttered quip: "Definitely, and with a great ass." He assumed I had not heard him.

Naturally, this was off-putting and made me feel uncomfortable. I was there to get my job done and to be taken seriously. I could have spoken up and demanded an apology. In fact, the project leader, who had also overheard the comment, later took me aside and told me that I needed to take action against the partner for saying such a crass thing. He said if someone said it to his wife, he would be very angry.

But I didn't take any action. The fact of the matter was this: I did not want to harm the partner's career and professional image. I liked him, and, while his comment certainly reeked of internalized sexism, I fully believed that he'd meant no offense. The last thing I wanted was to damage his reputation by presenting a petty complaint. There were many situations with clients and senior colleagues where something offensive or inappropriate was said; if I tried to avoid everyone who said something sexist or offensive to me, I would not have many people left to work with.

I, of course, do not condone such behavior. But I left the matter alone. The project manager thought less of me because of this. I continued to work with the same partner right up until I left the firm, at which point he wrote me an outstanding letter of recommendation. And this partner never said anything else offensive to me. I think he understood it was inappropriate without me mentioning anything. He also brought me as the key presenter to meetings with his top clients, even though I was still relatively junior. He was my raving fan within the firm. I kept my focus on what mattered. I knew to never lose sight of my objective: What matters is the work, delivering value for my clients and my firm, and if you can get it done, you'll often receive your desired results. And even if you don't, you will know you did everything you could to add value, and you are someone of whom you can be proud. The lesson taught to me here is that it's important not to become offended or hostile and to see a person as a whole, versus just paying attention to their one lapse in judgement or one bad quality. Rather than avoiding this partner I chose to continue working with him. And I truly believe, based on his actions, that he deeply valued me as a business professional. As I said, because of him I was the main presenter for top clients of the firm on number of occasions. I did not know of any other person at my level, or even one and two levels higher, who had the exposure to senior clients I had.

Discrimination because of my accent and where I was born was also abundant, and quite frankly much more hurtful. This is because discrimination related to having an accent is focused on you not being enough. And the two fears every human has, and I am no exception, are: what if they are not enough, and if they are not enough, they will not be loved, they will not belong, and they will be alone.

One story will be a great illustration of accent discrimination. There was an internal training I was once attending on how to present to clients. One of the more senior people in the group stood up and said that if she hears someone speaking with an accent, she does not even listen to them. And she was sitting across from me knowing full well that I speak with an accent. In fact, I think I was the only person in the room who hadn't spoken English their whole life. She was also a person who would be present in performance evaluations for my level at that time. I did not say a word, but I noted that as a potential disadvantage I would have to actively manage going forward with this manager.

Discrimination is something that comes with the territory when you are a woman or any kind of minority. At least it is still the case at the time of writing this. Not everything is personal, and rational attempts at educating someone aren't always effective or a good use of your limited time. This is especially important when it comes to building a bridge between yourself and a client. Leave your ego at the door and approach every situation with a positive attitude.

Furthermore, I think there's something to be said for how we let other people influence our own dignity and self-respect. I believed in myself. I presented myself with complete honesty, proud to be the hard worker that I was—and still am. Other people's words, however misguided, could never inhibit me, so long as I would not let it. People respect you when you respect yourself. That's a lesson that I've been learning all my life.

And in fact, if you are a minority, and you are outstanding despite all the discrimination, there will be many people looking up to you, learning from you, and emulating you. It gives you a chance to be a great leader for all the people who are discriminated against as well, or feel they are inferior in some way. Show them that success and contribution is possible regardless if you are a woman or a man, if you speak perfect English or speak with a thick accent to the point that people have to ask you to repeat yourself, if you were born in a prosperous country in a prestigious family or you are a Soviet Union baby, like me, born in a very poor family at the time with no roof over your head.

Sometimes you can benefit from being a minority. It's not always a liability. And I think you need to take advantage of those opportunities. For example, I know there were some clients who preferred to work with me before they even knew the value I could deliver because I was a woman and they liked having me around. I know some clients, even females, preferred to work with me because I speak with an accent, and they are tired of everyone speaking the same way; they want variety and many people told me that. They told me how much they love my accent because it's different.

So, if you are a minority, play the cards you are given. If you can benefit from being a minority in certain situations, use it. Like I used it by finding one project in the entire consulting practice that could greatly benefit from my knowledge of the Russian language and culture. And I was the only one with that knowledge. We are all given a set of assets. What worked for me is leaving my ego at the door and leveraging what I had.

My time working in South Africa was truly incredible and helped me on the road to becoming the person I am today. However, I knew even then that it wasn't where I was meant to stay. I had already made significant progress. Within two years, I was promoted three times. If you're at all familiar with the consulting environment, you know just how fast that is. Furthermore, I was told I was on track to be nominated for the next promotion within six months to a year at the time of my departure, as the result of my track record, including a very successful key engagement I'd managed to turn around. But I knew that it was time for me to leave. To succeed in a major western economy, I would need to earn a Master of Business Administration degree—an MBA. And not just any MBA, either: I wanted to study at the best school possible. I wanted to learn; I wanted my degree to mean something and to equip me with the tools necessary to fulfill my potential by making the highest possible level of contribution.

I made my move to Canada. I successfully finished my undergraduate work and began looking at potential graduate schools. I wasted no time: On the same day as my last exam for my undergraduate degree, I also took a shot at the Graduate Management Admission Test. The GMAT, as it's called, is an exam designed to evaluate various skills, including mathematics and written English—both of which were still weak points for me. Somewhat predictably, my initial score was far from impressive.

But I was not disheartened. I believed in my ability to figure it out and to work as hard as it took.

For six weeks, I buckled down to study, while simultaneously working to pay the bills by joining another international consulting firm in Toronto. I put all my energy into the work that I needed to do to take my next big step in life. Considering how far I had come, I had no choice but to plow forward at full speed.

The result? When I retook the GMAT, my score doubled. Not only that–I had also made the biggest improvement ever recorded over such a short period of time according to my friends. I am not particularly proud of this, because it meant I was starting off such a low base.

Standardized testing is one very easy way to compare yourself to your peers, but it's important to know that you should be very careful about choosing who your peers are. As a general rule, people tend to rise to the level of those around them. Personally, aside from my family and a few very close friends, my peer group consists of very senior and accomplished people who are purpose driven and with whom I work to create powerful programs, books, coaching, and other resources for our clients. They are usually ex-partners of consulting firms like BCG, McKinsey etc., CEOs, successful authors, and other business leaders. If you surround yourself with people you admire, you'll improve yourself little by little, every single day. Emulation is one of the most powerful forms of growth. Watch, listen, and learn, and you may very well find yourself on par with the best of the best much faster than you expect. Proximity is power.

With the GMAT conquered, I was free to apply to a business school. I didn't make my decision lightly; I knew that my whole future depended on the quality of the degree that I would be obtaining, and it had to be done in a way that I could handle financially. I ultimately decided to attend Richard Ivey Business School, which provided an entirely case-based program that had famously shaped all sorts of successful leaders. I picked Ivey despite winning full scholarships to other two-year program schools. I knew that case-based lessons were the right thing for me because they are effective in honing your decision-making ability. They demand complete and total dedication, along with an ability to see the big picture and identify the ripples effect that occur because of any given action. It was also the hardest school in Canada to get into and the most prestigious. I also picked this program because it was one year long rather than two, making it easier to handle financially. I sold my house in South Africa to pay for an MBA. Even so, there was a point during MBA when I only had $76 in my bank account. I was once again counting coins to see if I could buy lunch. I knew that if I graduated with straight As at the top MBA school in Canada my family and I would have a completely different future, and I will have more opportunities to contribute.

I worked day in and day out, forcing myself to read every single word that was assigned to me. Whenever I found the time to engage in extracurricular activities, I made sure that they were also beneficial to my future career path. I was both president of the public sector club and editor-in-chief of the public sector journal. At times I pushed myself too far. I fainted during a recruiting event and would have hit my head on the concrete floor if one of the executives from recruiting firm did not catch me.

Adversity can be seen as a vessel for self-improvement. To be a leader, you'll need to face all sorts of challenges, some of which may seem insurmountable. The thing to remember is that you're always growing, even if you fail every so often. Facing pushback is a sign that you're making valuable changes. Keep your chin up, keep trying, and keep believing in yourself. That's the key to taking on even the most arduous of tasks.

HONESTY TOWARD OTHERS, INTEGRITY TOWARD ONESELF

At one point, my finance professor offhandedly asked me about my post-graduation plans. He suggested that, instead of consulting, I should give banking a try. He said I had a great mind for a career in finance.

And so, I did just that, albeit for a shorter period than my professor had likely hoped. The interview process during my MBA was particularly painful because I did not yet have a permanent residence. So, companies were interested in me based on my application, but they were not able to sponsor me as it was not a part of their hiring process. I knew that was the case, but I also knew that at the end of the day, something would work out. Despite struggling with the hiring process because I did not have a permanent residence, only a study visa, I was also dedicated to remaining true to my values. But life kept on testing me. As an example, one excellent bank seemed ready to hire me as an investment banker on the condition that they were my first choice. The interviewer all but stated this outright; they repeatedly asked me whether it was the case, giving me plenty of room to amend my answer—which was that the bank was one of my top choices. I refused to be dishonest, even if nobody was personally harmed. I needed to trust myself and my ethics above all else. You only know you are truly a person with values if you are willing to leave money on the table to adhere to your values.

My real first choice ended up being just as eager to take me on. I was offered a position in the first interview and accepted it without a second thought. They were taking a risk to hire me because they also did not have approval to sponsor someone for permanent residency, so they hired me based on the hope that my permanent residence would be received in time. I did receive my PR before the start day, but it was a stressful journey to get there.

The interview was the best experience I had related to this bank. It all went downhill from there. Though I formed some wonderful relationships during my time at the bank, I had trouble finding any fulfillment in the work itself, and very quickly I came to realize that it wasn't the right path for me. Corporate banking work was very formulaic, and therefore less challenging and rewarding than the intricate problem-solving that had been central to earning my MBA and my consulting career. Despite this, I was promoted rapidly but chose to leave. I was also very different from all my colleagues. They could not understand why I would take one week of vacation time to work on an article. They could not understand why I was reading so much, why I was so interested in constantly learning and growing. I was like a fish out of water in that environment.

To be frank, while my clients loved me, while I was managing a portfolio of over 1 billion dollars, while I was more senior than quite possibly any of my former MBA classmates at that time, while in banking, I lived a life of quiet desperation. But I felt I had to stay long enough to make it worthwhile for the people who hired me—one VP, specifically. The moment I received an email from him, almost two years into my career with that bank, that he left to join a competitor, I knew I had to get out as soon as possible.

I ended up landing a consulting position through a conversation with a partner from a major firm. It was the first offer I received to leave the bank, and I took it because I couldn't spend any longer at the bank, even though it wasn't the type of consulting that I had been hoping to go back to. I applied myself with every ounce of my energy, working day in and day out. I didn't receive much satisfaction or joy necessary to sustain so much effort, and while I had enough mental fortitude to press on, shortly after I was staffed on two projects full-time, my body could not take it any longer.

I became sick—very sick. For the first time since my allergic reaction to a vaccine as a teenager, I was completely indisposed. My hair was falling out, and I had inflammation in my brain. The only way I would make it was through immediate intervention; otherwise, there was a good chance I would not recover.

During those days, I once again found myself confronting how little time I quiet likely had left. Though my condition wasn't labeled as terminal, it might as well have been; the prospect of recovery was a big question mark. If this was the end of my story, what did that mean? What was I working so hard for? What had I contributed to the world? Whom did I help? Did I help the right people? Would all my work, suffering, and sacrifices be for nothing? What would happen to my family without me?

I knew that, once again, I needed to make a change. It was time to point myself in the right direction, once and for all.

This is when I dedicated myself to FIRMSconsulting full-time.

FIRMSconsulting is different from so many other companies because it exists for the sake of making a difference. I had proven to myself that I could accomplish anything if I set my mind to it, and I wanted other people not only to feel the same way but also to have the necessary skills, approaches, techniques, playbooks, and required mindset to be able to do it. This was my opportunity to ensure just that.

Building FIRMSconsulting was not easy, and it's an ongoing process. Resources and staff were, and still are, limited, but what we did have was a solid goal: We wanted to help people build powerful skill sets so they could unlock their full potential, solve meaningful problems that positively impact the world, and have a bigger life than they ever thought was possible for them.

Many people don't know this about FIRMSconsulting but we have a deep reach globally. Our podcast channels like Strategy Skills are often top 5 ranked career podcasts in India, China, Singapore, Saudi Arabia, UAE, Denmark etc. We built the largest strategy, consulting practice building, and leadership on-demand video training library in the world at StrategyTraining.com and run the largest publishing house for business strategy. We have a global reach with professionals around the world using our material daily. Some clients tell us that they literally sleep with our books under their pillow. Others tell us that if they came across our work while they were in high school, they would be the president of their country by now. Even the executive committee members of some of the largest consulting firms and companies use our work.

Our core philosophy is that anyone can achieve great things if they persevere and have access to resources to build powerful skill sets and mindsets. Our mission is to be the intelligence that powers professionals and entrepreneurs around the world to have a level of contribution and financial peace they never thought was possible for them before they came across FIRMSconsulting.

Running your own business may sound easier than working for someone else, but I quickly confirmed what I suspected, that wasn't at all the case. In the early stages, for the business to survive and become stable, I had to—and to a large degree still continue to—serve as an operator rather than an owner to keep costs down, build the right culture, maintain quality standards, and ensure our customers and clients are well taken care of.

In the early days, you are usually your own complete team. For me, that meant that I was our director, videographer, light designer, content creator, video and audio editor, account manager for key clients, coach, customer service representative, head of partnerships, website designer, development and optimization person, set creator, graphic designer, food delivery person, copywriter, makeup artist, podcast booking agent, podcast host and everything in-between. Calling it exhausting would be an understatement. Shoots would run for days at a time, and I often struggled to stay awake by the time I was performing the finishing touches because at some point, adrenaline is just no longer enough to keep you going. You are not a machine: you need food, sleep, and rest.

I once passed out from exhaustion hours before we were shooting a video program for our streaming service. I made a deal with the team that I would go to the hospital if they continued the shoot. We were not going to cancel.

The doctor at the hospital showed me what to do if I ever feel I am about to faint. I had to sit and put my head between my knees. She explained that your body gets overwhelmed and, like a computer, shuts down. What she showed me works. I never fainted from exhaustion again. If I ever feel it is coming, I sit down, put my head between my knees, and it goes away.

Still, I persevered. By now, I was well-versed in the art of resilience, and the importance of FIRMSconsulting's mission gives me strength to keep pressing on. That belief in the company, in our values, and in my own ability to do the right thing, was what led me to where we are today.

Wherever I saw a problem, I looked for a solution, no matter how painful that solution may be for me personally, such as taking on yet an additional set of responsibilities because we did not have funds to hire someone tested and competent. I was managing all corners of production, from content planning to our relationships with ex-McKinsey, BCG *et al.* partners and CEOs, to the cinematography of our shoots. I also managed post-production and worked closely with clients to see how we could help them even more. Due to the struggles I faced as a child in Russia, and later as a young adult, I had become an exceptionally frugal person, and I applied my money-saving techniques to the entire company; especially if it was my expenses, such as booking the cheapest possible flights, renting the cheapest possible cars, or skipping meals.

Through these years of frugality and back breaking work, FIRMSconsulting grew into the media organization that it is today. And now, looking back on the fruits of my labor, getting messages from our readers, customers and clients from all over the world about how FIRMSconsulting helped them dramatically change their life, and their family's lives, I finally feel the sense of fulfillment and sense of knowing that I am doing the work I am supposed to be doing–something I had been seeking all of my life. Ever since my childhood, I've been pursuing ways to leave a positive impact on the world, and that's exactly what FIRMSconsulting is able to do to a much larger degree than what my previous positions in consulting or banking allowed me to accomplish. I consider the impact FIRMSconsulting was able to achieve so far to be my greatest achievement to date, and, God willing, I'll continue to foster the company's growth and impact until my last day on earth.

I still work extremely hard and actively try to build a stronger and stronger team around myself, so we can do more for our clients, customers, and our broader community around the world. I also found a better sense of balance in my life. I now have an amazing team so I no longer have to do everything. It made me a more effective leader for the company because I can focus on building for the future; more time to think allowed me to better see where I should take FIRMSconsulting next and what we need to do to help our clients even more. Today, many people rely on me to continue doing my work: clients, employees, family, friends, and even people whom I haven't yet met, but whose lives FIRMSconsulting transformed or will be able to transform.

In reaching this point, I've made my fair share of mistakes. I'm immensely grateful that I was able to withstand the hard times and for being able to contribute to the world in this way.

OWNING YOUR LIFE

In 2017, for the first time in a decade, I found myself back home in Russia. It was a three-week trip, and I filled it with time spent alongside my family, whom I love dearly: my mother, my father, my twin brothers, and my then-pregnant sister Nailia, her husband and his family. We visited all sorts of places that reminded me of my childhood, including my school and my kindergarten, but the most emotional one was my grandmother's house. It had been sold many years ago, back when she first grew severely ill, and no small number of changes had been made to it since then. Though the house was nearly unrecognizable, from what I could see from the street, it was still deeply moving to look at it and, if just for a second, feel like I was back there with my grandmother playing on the street. I remember that one time when we played "baba sela na goroh I skazala oh." The rules of the game are simple. I had to say those words and then fall back, and my grandmother would catch me. It was cold outside, everything around was white from the snow, and it was dark. I remember I was afraid to fall but my grandmother promised me she would catch me, and she, of course, did. One of the saddest parts of life is when the person who gave you the best memories, themselves become a memory.

The memories that came back to me over the course of that trip weren't all good ones. Though my parents tried their hardest, they were far from perfect, and our family's circumstances meant that my siblings and I all had very difficult childhoods. We faced poverty, hunger, discrimination, and more. But we never stopped loving and caring for one another, despite physical and emotional abuse I had to go through as the oldest child.

While living my life so far away from my family was a sacrifice I would never wish for anyone, leaving Russia and working as hard as I did, I've been able to be in a position to cover my family's key medical expenses and other needs, and provide career opportunities for anyone within my family who wanted or needed them. And Nailia, the tiny human I could hold with my one hand as a 9-year-old, became a crucial and brilliantly talented member of the FIRMSconsulting team.

Those of us who aspire to be great leaders must be willing to make sacrifices for the good of others. It takes guts to make tough choices, but as leaders, it's something that we need to do. Our job is to take on the hardest of tasks, even those that may seem impossible. As much as I struggled against adversity on my path to building a career, and later a business, I've been rewarded with the possibility of a better future for many people.

Your story probably doesn't look like mine. There's power in that: Just as my unique experiences led me to success, I know that yours can do the same. We are all unique human beings with unique things to offer the world. No one can be you, and no one can contribute in a way that you can.

I also strongly believe that investing in yourself is the single best investment that you can make. Spend time considering your values, and ask yourself questions: What do you want in life? What are you trying to avoid? What's possible for you, and what isn't? And if you think it's not possible for you, is it true? Or is it a lie that you've been telling yourself for so long that you now take it as a fact? If it is attainable, and if you believe it is aligned with your purpose, do your best to achieve it. If you believe that you can build a multimillion-dollar business that helps improve the lives of countless people around the world, then you can. But if you don't believe something is possible for you, you've lost before giving yourself a chance to begin.

It's inevitable that you're going to struggle. Many things that are worth having require sacrifice. Great achievements come at great costs, and you need to be willing to pay the price that comes with your chosen path. Love the problems that come with your dream. That is why I was able to live without money to buy lunch or be rejected from every job I applied to for eight months and not give up. And there were many jobs I was rejected from, hundreds and hundreds, because I applied literally for every job I could qualify for on the local jobs site.

This isn't a matter of compromise, but rather one of acceptance. Don't fight the problems that accompany your dreams. Instead, learn to love them. Your dream is a package; trouble comes with the package. For example, if you want to be a parent, love the trouble that comes with it: sleepless nights, additional expenses, less free time, changing diapers, and more worries.

If your dream is to build a business that will create a better future for millions of clients around the world, you need to make peace with the difficulties that come with it. You'll need to sacrifice free time, accept a tremendous amount of responsibility, and maybe, like me, move far away from your home and family to have an opportunity to make this dream a reality.

Would I have ever been able to build FIRMSconsulting if I stayed in Samara? Would I have ever be able to lead the organization to the point where it helps millions of people around the world if I never left everything behind and started the onerous journey in a strange country, barely speaking the local language? All of these were necessary challenges that accompanied pursuing a worthwhile vision for myself, my family, and my future clients and finding what I could do for the world.

I was rejected from hundreds of jobs. Money was scarce, meals weren't always easy to come by, and my health—even my abilities such as the capacity to remember things—often seemed to be working against me. Countless times, people whom I trusted and admired told me that I couldn't achieve my dreams.

Now, I strive to approach every day in a state of absolute certainty, with a dedicated focus on contributing at the highest level possible. When you're sure of your ability to work things out for the better, when you truly care about the best interests of your team members and your clients, and when you focus on doing work that holds value well beyond your ability to succeed, many people will follow you by instinct. People want to have a leader, but only as long as that leader truly has their best interest at heart.

Being in the right mental state by continuously working on breaking down your limiting beliefs and helping your team and clients do the same is also critical to being an effective leader. It may be hard to achieve but remember: Your mind is your greatest tool. The key to success lies in always taking the next step. You can't fail if you do not give up. It's how you manage adversity that will determine your success or failure. If you're on the wrong path, it's never too late to start in a new direction. You're the only person capable of shaping your destiny and giving a purpose to your life.

As challenging as it's been, I'm grateful for the life that I've led so far. My many struggles have put everything in perspective, and I know now that I'm capable of achieving almost anything if I set my mind to it. I believe the same is true for you, and for everyone else in the world. Nobody should have to settle for a life of quiet desperation or a barely content life. Everyone has the potential to go beyond what society may have intended for them.

If you are reading this and you are going through similar experiences as I did, my message to you is not to stop. Maintain persistence, remind yourself of your purpose, and never, ever give up. If you do your best every day, demand of yourself to grow continuously, and never give up, you are giving yourself a good chance to make it. It will not be easy. If it was easy, everyone would make a significant contribution to the world. You will hate the difficult moments, but you will likely one day realize they were a blessing that allowed you to be the person you are today. They will become your emotional shield. They will become something that makes you believe you can deal with any situation because you have dealt with harder things and managed to get through them. They will make you wiser and give you the ability to see patterns others don't see.

And along the way, what you need is a strong 'why.' I believe it is the one true source of persistence. You need to try to connect with why you were born: What is your mission here? Who needs you? Because there will be times when things will get tough, and it may seem like it would not be such a bad idea to just give up and settle for a barely content life—for a 'normal' life. And you will need your 'why' to give you enough persistence to get through those difficult times.

Persistence by itself, however, will not be sufficient. You need clarity on the goal you want to achieve. You may not know the complete picture of your vision, but you need to know an approximate direction. Fulfilling your mission in life often feels like going up a dark staircase, and you are only shown the next step. And sometimes, you take the next step and realize you are going in the wrong direction, and you step down a couple of steps and start climbing in a different direction. But, from my experience, you will be shown the next step, and that is all you need. Along the way you will need to learn from your own experiences while adopting the best practices from people who have already achieved what you are trying to achieve and are willing to teach you.

I wake up each morning and still work almost every waking moment. Weekends, public holidays, and evenings. The good news is, now it's my choice. I have the privilege to do what I feel I was born to do—helping people around the world transform their careers, businesses, and lives. I do not want anyone anywhere in the world to settle for a life of quiet desperation and a barely content life. I want you to aspire to and have the skills for more than what society had intended for you.

That's my 'why.' To be a great leader, you need to find yours.

AUTHOR BIO

Kris Safarova is a Wall Street Journal, USA Today and Amazon bestselling author, and founder and CEO of FIRMSconsulting.com & StrategyTraining.com.

She manages a portfolio of companies, which includes the world's largest strategy and consulting business-building video training platforms, StrategyTraining.com and FIRMSconsulting.com, a publishing business, and she studied under Roger Love, the most eminent voice coach in the world, to become a reputed and certified executive presence and speaking coach.

Kris also manages two iTunes career podcasts ranked in the top ten in many countries- "Strategy Skills" and "Case Interviews & Management Consulting."

She holds an MBA from Ivey Business School in Canada, where she was on the dean's list and graduated with highest distinction, and a degree in economics from UNISA, where she graduated *cum laude*. Prior to her MBA, Kris worked in management consulting, and following her MBA she worked as a corporate banker and managed a portfolio worth more than US$1 billion before returning to consulting.

Before entering the consulting industry, Kris was a master classical concert pianist and official music representative of the Russian Federation, who toured Europe.

Connect With Kris: FIRMSconsulting.com and StrategyTraining.com

Receive a Gift From Kris: Get your copy of an accompanying guide for this book "14 Little Known Communication Approaches to Turn You Into an Influential and Impactful Leader" here: www.firmsconsulting.com/executive-presence.

CHAPTER 2

Innovative Leadership and the Critical Path

BY VINCENT SAMAT

I'VE ALWAYS BEEN MOTIVATED by the desire to take on new opportunities. Whether it be originating new products, expanding on existing products, addressing client niches, driving growth within various client segments, or mentoring people toward excellence in their own positions, the appeal of something fresh and challenging is enough to capture my attention and efforts.

Due to this drive, I've been able to lead a varied career at large global American and European firms, as well as several smaller firms. I currently lead a product team in capital markets within a business-to-business context. My work and the work of my team includes product development and product design, product pricing strategy, putting products into production, internal and external product marketing, overall product management, and occasionally product sales. There are several unique challenges in leading a team of high performers to create value for clients in a fast-paced, high-pressure environment, especially considering that we have to make split-second decisions that can bring in or cost seven figures or more.

Growing into this position was the result of a long journey. Looking back on how far I've come, there are several things that I wish I could have known from the beginning in order to augment and accelerate my journey. By sharing these lessons with you, the reader, I hope to be able to give you that extra boost that will elevate you to achieve your own success and personal growth, while also inspiring you to aid the growth of others.

THE CRITICAL PATH TO CREATING VALUE FOR CLIENTS

When my career was first beginning to take off, I often found myself believing that I had to know everything all the time. After all, I was here to serve clients, right? I initially considered my role to be a reactive one, and I entered client meetings with the understanding that I was there simply to present products or implement exactly what clients were asking for. I also wasn't sure how to determine what information was useful. Was I supposed to be the one talking most of the time? How could I showcase every possibility of the entire product suite without losing the client's interest?

While I had been exposed to various approaches toward optimizing value in these interactions, the turning point for me was a specific client meeting. I was accompanied by an experienced salesperson, and I had the chance to witness firsthand the subtleties of their approach: They turned the meeting from a potentially one-sided pitch into a genuine *conversation*. They spoke back and forth, expressing concerns and constraints. Rather than feeling the need to present a broad range of information, I was therefore able to prioritize listening and learning. When I opened my mouth, it was only to ask targeted questions, gathering more data that I could use to assemble an effective solution to the client's needs.

After the meeting, I took my time processing everything that I had learned, and eventually was able to develop a product prototype that was customized to the particular client. Though I didn't think of it as such at the time, this was the first time that I made use of something that I later called the *critical path*. Through the use of this critical path, I learned how you can transform a small client into one of your largest.

What is the critical path? Put most simply, it's a path that directly addresses the concerns and problems facing a client, rather than attempting to fit their unique situation into a pre-rendered product design. It's quite antithetic to the 'one-size-fits-all' philosophy. Calling it a 'path' is not entirely accurate; rather than a journey from point A to point B, the critical path is a cycle that begins and ends with the client, with the product team working in the middle. This cycle often needs to be repeated several times over in order to refine aspects of the product. The result? A clean, smooth, and effective route of customer service that fully satisfies the client's needs and concerns.

A journey down the critical path will require the usage of two main skills: listening and asking. In other words: Be prepared for a lot of conversation and critical thinking.

More than anything, the question you should be asking is 'Why?' Why does a client have a particular concern? Why are they interested in specific product features? Why do they feel it necessary to operate within their given timeline? None of this should ever be posed as a challenge to the client; in fact, one of the most important things to do in these meetings is to remain open-minded, never projecting your thoughts and wishes onto the client's perspective. Instead, think of yourself as conducting research, or even an interview. Try to pull out as much information as possible so that your ensuing work can be optimally effective.

'Pull' is a key word here. Think of it in opposition to its antonym, 'push.' A pull-based method is driven by the client's problems, needs, and concerns: It parses the specifics of a situation, identifying the needs and issues that a product will need to possess. Zoom in on the biggest issues on the client's mind and try to provide solutions that will be the most impactful in addressing those issues. A push-based method, on the other hand, involves the pushing or forcing of an existing product onto a client, who may or may not be able to make use of it. When you focus only on pitching your products, you're instantly narrowing your possibility of success.

You may find that you naturally gravitate toward a push-based line of action. This is perfectly natural; people are more comfortable when we stick to what we know, rather than opening ourselves up to ambiguity. However, there are some easy ways to combat this and gear yourself more toward a pull-based method.

For starters, bring two people to your meeting: the salesperson covering the client and a well-seasoned product person who can focus on listening to the client and addressing their concerns. While the meeting is happening, pay attention to whether the salesperson or the client is doing the majority of the talking, and whether concerns are being dismissed rather than productively confronted. Stay flexible and responsive; don't be afraid to deviate from the preconceived pitch.

Lastly, be sure to keep in mind that the client's concerns will likely go beyond the product. Think about customer service, implementation, internal approval, economic conditions, and so on. Lateral thinking is key to the critical path. If you broaden your scope of consideration and incorporate all the possible nuances and repercussions of each choice you make, you'll be well on your way to finding a truly effective product solution that provides the best possible customer experience.

HIGH PRODUCERS

A tenet of good leadership is the ability to become a high producer, and to then turn others into high producers, and eventually into leaders. High producers typically produce multiples of other producers and/ or relevant benchmarks (for example: revenue targets). I've gotten to know several high producers throughout my professional life, and they possess a variety of characteristics and strategies, driven first and foremost by proactivity and persistence. One of them prioritized the creation of customized products, resulting in a longer time frame that garnered tremendously effective results. Another focused on a small number of very large transactions with valuable clients. A third made use of consistency, steadily re-engaging clients with ideas and themes every single day, then adjusting products as needed.

High producers operate through action plans. Proactivity is key. At any given moment, they'll have designated goals for their day, along with a plan for how to achieve those goals. They'll also have clear weekly, monthly, and yearly action plans. In order to be a high producer, you should know exactly where you stand in relation to your long-term goals.

Strong relationships are also incredibly important in this area. Focusing on relationships with key clients while maintaining awareness of the critical path is of the utmost importance.

While all of these commonalities are important to keep in mind, the best way that you can learn from high producers is by observing them on your own. Identify the high producers in your area and study their methods. Consider their drive, their perceived incentives, their approach toward serving clients, and their strategies when it comes to team play. On some occasions, you may find that they create friction within their organization, largely due to the perceived incentives under which their work culture operates. However, recall the importance of adjustment and flexibility—not just between salesperson and client, but also within a company itself. You may not always be best advised to precisely emulate the behaviors of the high producers around you, but the potential to learn from their methods of driving business is nonetheless extraordinary.

In my personal experience, I always made an effort to identify and partner with high producers in each firm. Since I was often moving between firms in order to embrace new challenges, I was able to use my various sources of knowledge to identify strengths, weaknesses, and untapped opportunities. For instance, I might find that high producers in my current firm were always selling X Product, whereas my previous role had shown me more success in the sales of Y Product. Asking 'why' and breaking down these differences was a remarkably effective way to understand what it truly means to be a high producer.

When it comes to refining your own business model, there are a number of considerations to keep in mind. One way to organize your considerations is by envisioning a two-by-two matrix juxtaposing volume versus margin. Which mix is optimal for your organization—low volume and high margin or high volume and low margin? Maybe you depend on a large amount of small repeat business that consumes little bandwidth—in which case you'll want to look at the extent to which that can become automated. Or maybe you're on the other end of the spectrum, and your focus is on customizing larger pieces of business in order to create a higher value for the customer. Is the rest of the organization well-equipped to start doing more customized business? Which approach will offer you the most growth opportunities based on what you know about your situation and resources? Which approach is more resilient to difficult times? It may take a while to sort through all of these considerations, but a truly effective business model will always be worth the trouble.

INNOVATION: UNICORN, PEGASUS, CHIMERA, AND BELLEROPHON

When it comes to your actual product, many people misunderstand the meaning of 'innovation.' Innovation can be considered to be the act of creating something entirely original, something that will outdo the largest competitors in your field, something that will create a new field entirely—but the truth is that it's much more than that.

The idea of push versus pull comes back into play here. When you try to come up with "the next great thing" out of nowhere, you're pushing to create something out of nothing. When you prioritize pulling out existing issues and addressing them via small modifications and customizations, on the other hand, you may find it much easier to be productive, efficient... and yes, innovative.

In addition to the difficulty of conjuring up a new product from scratch, you may run the risk of quickly losing your innovation advantage. In my field, there's little intellectual property protection for new products, resulting in a lack of barriers to entry between yourself and your competitors. A product may take months to develop, only for it to be copied in five minutes. The way to avoid this? Maintain niche differences from your competitor. Focus on *all* aspects of the value chain for the client, not just your product itself; customer service, for example, provides grounds for all sorts of innovation.

I was once invited to a client meeting by a risk manager, in which the client was seemingly focused on keeping their products simple and standard. I was initially under the impression that my customization-based approach would be useless in this situation, since the client did not seem to have needs for specific tweaks. However, that turned out not to be the case at all. By expanding my understanding of potential innovation, I came to realize that we could actually broaden our offering with a different angle: a simple standard product, but with a different packaging. Was the result flashy and game-changing? Certainly not—but it was *effective*.

Another time, I similarly found myself working with a product that was far from new or customizable. Noting this, I still continued to search for anything that could optimize the product and our company's relationship with the clients who used that product. Through this, I discovered that the popularity of the product had a tendency to rise when certain market conditions were being met. This enabled me to predict the times during which clients were most likely to engage with the product. I then proceeded to monitor the situation of the market on a daily basis. When I found that the favorable conditions were met, I notified the salesperson, who was then able to take advantage of the corresponding uptick in interest.

These experiences, among others, helped me to sophisticate my understanding of what exactly defines innovation. Is it most synonymous with differentiation? Disruption? Revolution? All of these concepts are deeply intertwined, but innovation at its core is about moving forward. If you're employing new ideas that will help facilitate your relationship with the changing world around you for the benefit of your clients, you're an innovator. This skill is more necessary than ever in the 21st century, with technological developments and socioeconomic conditions fluctuating at an unprecedented pace.

Since it has so much to do with the interplay between ourselves and our surroundings, innovation is also highly subjective by nature. To frame this in the context of the business world, imagine introducing a client to a preexisting product for the first time. To them, that's an act of innovation. Though it may not seem that way, you did indeed create something new—but, instead of a product, it was a *connection*.

Knowing all of this, try to examine potential innovation—no matter how big or small—throughout the entire value chain. Client prospection, customer service, product offering, IT, internal processes, distribution channels, business models, and diversity of profiles are all areas where you may very well find an opportunity to innovate. These opportunities don't need to be dramatic or complex. Keep refining the processes that have already been developed, and you'll find that you operate in a way that fosters innovation in an increasingly efficient and effective manner. You'll also be able to position yourself more distinctly against your competitors. Even the word 'competitor' becomes less than accurate at this point, because, in a way, you won't be competing at all. Instead of doing something *better* than top competitors in the market, you're doing something *different*. Individuality drives value like nothing else.

Let's take a moment to review the most important takeaways regarding the innovative process. In bullet point form, they look something like this:

- Use the 'pull' method to engage with *all* stakeholders in order to identify and understand issues and constraints. This is tremendously easier than trying to conjure fully realized ideas out of thin air.
- Don't forget about the concept of the critical path. Look at each problem as its own entity, with particular needs that are unlikely to be met by preexisting solutions.
- Keep an eye out for missed opportunities. You may be met with phrases such as "It's not possible," "It's never been done," or "It's never going to work." Internal resistance to change is an innovation killer. Instead of giving value to these assumptions, always take a moment to think about *why*. If something hasn't been done before, that doesn't automatically make it impossible. Think outside the box and embrace the value of unexpected change.

Lastly, and perhaps most importantly, keep an open mind. Business opportunities are all around us. I personally find that my best ideas come to me during quiet periods of transition, bereft of life's usual distractions: an evening commute, a mountain hike, a ride down an empty ski slope. Other times, innovation can emerge from what seems to be a trivial question from a team member. Stay alert and curious, and you'll find that our world is absolutely teeming with the potential for innovation

MANAGING TIME AND SETTING PRIORITIES UNDER HIGH PRESSURE

My typical morning can look something like this:

- **9:45 a.m.** I receive an email from Salesperson 1 asking for a marketing presentation.
- **9:48 a.m.** An instant message arrives through the internal messaging system from Salesperson 2, asking whether we have any interesting products to show to clients today.
- **9:54 a.m.** Another email lands in my inbox, this time from Salesperson 3. They're asking for more information regarding a client meeting from last week as part of their follow-up process.
- **10:00 a.m.** I log into a conference call regarding the development of a new product with a team in Europe.
- **10:04 a.m.** I get an email requesting a product quote for Client A.
- **10:11 a.m.** Salesperson 4 stops by my desk to discuss our plans for Client B.
- **10:16 a.m.** I receive another email, this time asking for a product quote for Client C.
- **10:24 a.m.** My senior manager requests an update on delivering Product X for Client D.
- **10:36 a.m.** A member of our support team comes to me with questions on a client transaction that occurred yesterday.

- **10:42 a.m.** A risk manager (trader) asks for additional analysis on Product Y.

And that's just the first hour of the workday.

When you're dealing with such a fast-paced, high-pressure environment, day after day, you'll need to build a strategy for organizing and prioritizing your different tasks. If you get distracted by piles and piles of new tasks, you'll find yourself failing to make meaningful progress over time. Where do you find an opportunity to focus on new products, key clients, and so on?

Remember: The goal is to create value to the clients and to your organization. Your first step is to prioritize *results* over *activity*. Take a look at all of the projects that your team tackles in a given amount of time—perhaps a week or a month. Out of them all, which will have the most impact in both short-term and long-term timeframes? Be on the lookout for "scope creep," an issue in which your tasks are growing progressively more distant from the focus of your original mission. It may feel as though each bit of work naturally leads to the next, but you also need to keep track of the distance from your core objective, lest you end up miles away from it.

Once you've done this, track the actions of yourself and your team throughout the designated period of time. Make note of the different directions in which your team members are applying their efforts. Consider what you may need to do in order to correct your course and improve your productivity—and, of course, keep in mind that productivity isn't exclusively quantitative. Making gradual progress by evenly applying your efforts to your entire task list is almost always less valuable than concentrating on specific goals that will push a couple of projects over the finish line. Pick your priorities and stick to them.

In order for this to work, you'll need to master a skill that many people may struggle with: You need to learn how to say 'no.' You can't be everything to everyone and trying to do so runs the risk of resulting in universal mediocrity. Instead, identify tasks that may need to be dropped, and make sure that the sales and product teams are communicating openly about where their focus needs to lie. By minimizing extraneous work and evenly delegating what remains, you may find that your overall productivity increases significantly.

IT'S ALL ABOUT PEOPLE, PEOPLE, PEOPLE

When I was first getting started with my career, my background was based in quantitative academics. For a role in a quantitative business, this may seem ideal—and, in many ways, it was; a solid grip of mathematics can be key to understanding the nuances of financial markets. Nonetheless, my time in numeral-oriented academia also left me lacking a certain crucial skill set: I had yet to further develop my own people skills.

For a lot of us, an academic learning environment is a clinical and objective one. We receive assignments, we complete assignments, we receive feedback for assignments. Rinse and repeat. Once you enter the real world, though, you'll all too soon be faced with reality: People come first every single time. Take care of people, and they'll take care of business.

I, for one, learned this lesson the hard way. Several years ago, during a meeting, I ended up arguing with one particular salesperson. In retrospect, I can recognize that the topic itself was unimportant—writing this, I don't even remember a single detail about the subject matter. What I do remember is the sense of frustration that ensued. The salesperson in question shut me down firmly, and I expected to move on from there. I then realized the *personal* repercussions that would occur if I maintained my defiant attitude – attitude that I immediately dropped; and that salesperson has become a close friend ever since.

Another salesperson, one who had witnessed the conflict as it played out, later came to me with advice. That event was a 'Aha!' moment for me. They gently explained a simple fact that I've carried with me ever since: Internal friction of that kind will never have a productive outcome. I wasn't going to achieve any of my goals through argument. As a matter of fact, the more you argue your point, the less likely you are to get your way. For a long time, I had trouble understanding this; shouldn't I be prioritizing the outcome? An ideal product, idea, or implementation should come first and foremost... or so I thought.

Because of this, I did not apologize for my role in the initial argument at the time. Looking back, this was a memorable mistake. Never be afraid to say that you're sorry: Leave your ego at the door. Though it may not seem to be the case, this is actually more important than ever when it comes to leadership. When a leader lets it be known that they will not always be in the right, that makes things easier for their team as a whole. It establishes an understanding that nobody is expected to get things right 100% of the time. As a result, your team members will feel comfortable in embracing and addressing their mistakes rather than covering them up.

This connects back to the importance of seeking a mentor early in your career. Learning from another person will be more effective than studying any book. They'll teach you that doing your best is not always about having the best product or the best answer to every question. Real life isn't a math exam, and you don't need to score 100/100. Instead, look at each relationship in its own context. Sometimes, you need to say no. Sometimes, you won't get it right. Sometimes—in fact, a lot of the time—you'll need to make decisions that leave you unsatisfied.

And that's okay. More than okay, it's smart. It's what every good leader would do. If there's one thing to remember, it's this: Treat everyone inside the organization the same way you would treat your largest client.

BOUNCING BACK AFTER FAILURE

Here's something that nobody wants to hear: You're going to fail.

I don't mean that you're going to fail at everything, but you *are* going to fail at some things. The only way to avoid failure entirely is to not try in the first place—or not try hard enough. If you spend all your life within the constraints of your comfort zone, you'll never give yourself room to grow.

With this in mind, one of the most important things to learn is how to bounce back from your failures. Experimentation in the form of trial and error is integral to the process of taking on new challenges, especially when it comes to product development and adding value to clients.

Let me illustrate this by way of my own story.

The year 2009 was rough all around. The financial crisis was in full swing, and economic stability sounded like a pipe dream. I had just left a good, reliable position at a large firm, choosing instead to pursue a role at a smaller firm with more entrepreneurial prospects. Before long, my new firm closed, and I was left to job hunt late in the year—a process that was complicated even further by constraints with my work visa. I eventually managed to land at another small firm, only to be laid off less than two years later as part of a workforce reduction effort.

For the next five months, I remained unemployed. The pressure was on, and as a result, I worked harder than ever. I needed opportunities, and the only way that I was going to get them was by using all the time I had to network and explore my prospects. I was a risky candidate: My resume showcased a wide variation of roles in several different firms but gave no sign of specialized skills on my part.

I finally got a chance in a larger firm. To start with, I was given a number of product and client segments that were in need of reinvention with no one internally focusing on those. I had no idea how to generate business; no manual of instructions was handed to me. Yet, in the next year and a half, I gradually found ways to make it work. My only choice was to learn by experimenting, so I did just that, with the help of a few key people within the organization. The keyword here is grit: Develop that skill.

Since then, I've made it a priority to take on new challenges, both internal and external, especially whenever I feel that I've reached a plateau. This doesn't entail overloading myself with a plethora of unnecessary difficulties, but rather checking in with myself on a regular basis and identifying areas for personal improvement. As a leader, this is absolutely essential: There is no team growth without leadership growth, and new challenges are the main way to facilitate that. There's no point at which you'll be "good enough" to stop pushing yourself. In the absence of new challenges, skills don't plateau; they regress.

Another way to think about this is by looking at the differences between large organizations and start-ups. Large organizations tend to emphasize their ability to operate well-known ways of doing things, while large-scale experimentation could be considered risky. Start-ups, on the other hand, are all about experimentation. Tweaking, adjusting, and learning from mistakes are the main reliable way to test and develop a new product.

We often find ourselves held back by the fear of failure, but the truth is that failure isn't something that needs to be feared whatsoever. If you can take calculated risks and embrace the inevitability of disruption, you may find yourself making much larger and more effective strides in the development of your products and ideas. You'll never be 100% ready for the challenges that truly push you to grow. Stop putting them off and embrace the inevitability of doing an imperfect job. In the words of John Maxwell: "Fail early, fail often, but always fail forward."

SEEKING MENTORSHIP

As an extension of our universal fear of failure or showing weakness, people can find themselves reluctant to ask for help early on. In my most difficult times early in my career, I rarely sought advice from people with more experience than myself. This meant that I learned a lot of lessons the hard way. Failure-driven experimentation can be effective, but not necessary 100% of the time, as well as costly; sometimes, another person has already been there, and can help you along by sharing their own story. As a student, you're taught that relying on others at an exam is a form of cheating. In the real world, it becomes one of your most important tools.

Ask candid questions to trusted mentors, with intent. Why are you moving jobs? How do you negotiate compensation? How do you ask for a promotion? How will you know when the time is right to take on a new challenge? More experienced people may have the answers to these questions and more, and you gain nothing by denying yourself access to their knowledge. Identify the people who can serve as mentors to you and seek them out—*now*. Life moves faster than anyone expects, and waiting will do you no good.

On the other side of things, recognize that it's never too early for you to become a mentor as well as a mentee. Learning from one another is an exceptionally valuable way to navigate the most difficult parts of our lives. Take what you're given by others and offer to them what you can in turn.

SLOW DOWN

Slow down.

I mean that, of course, in a broad sense, but also an immediate one.

Now—right now—take a moment to slow down and reflect on how that feels.

Maybe you've been cruising your way through these lessons, or maybe you've taken the time to process each one individually. In either case, you can always make use of a checkpoint to pause and reassess. Does your current situation make sense in the context of your goals, or have you been barreling forward without regard to your direction?

Try practicing this on a regular basis. Put time aside from the daily grind and take a look at where you stand in relation to the big picture. In a fast-paced, high-pressure environment, it's easy to veer off course by getting caught in an activity-driven mindset of "doing stuff" rather than an outcome-driven mindset. Consider: What was the strategy? What was the goal? Are you still on track? Why did you select that strategy or goal initially? Should you adjust the strategy and come up with fresh ideas?

Sometimes, lessons are simple.

This is one of them.

Just slow down.

NAVIGATING THE MAZE OF ORGANIZATIONAL SILOS

One of the harder elements of leadership is the fact that you aren't always in control. That may sound contradictory but think about it for a moment: When you're responsible for a number of different individuals, a number of teams, or multiple business units, you'll almost always find that they each have their own agendas and their own ways of doing things. Because of this, they sometimes end up operating in ways that aren't optimal for your organization as a whole. These isolated, individual functions are often referred to as 'silos.'

Silos are almost never created and operated out of selfishness. As a matter of fact, subsects of companies often develop their own private goals and frameworks out of the desire to be as beneficial as possible to the larger organization. There's something of a paradox in play here: Every team is highly skilled at their own work, and every team is trying their best to improve the functions of the organization as a whole. If everyone's intentions are good, how can the outcome be suboptimal?

One of my own experiences demonstrates the core issue here. I once found myself dealing with a scenario in which a software team made a change without informing the larger company network. It was by all means a great feature: It was flexible, smart, and cleanly written.

However, the team that handled the interface didn't know that this was happening. As a result, the user interface broke the very next day when the product team attempted to use it. No particular step was a bad one, but the lack of overall cooperation transformed a great concept into a disruptive failure.

The fact of the matter is that it's impossible to understand the repercussions of any given action that a team decides to take. Business organizations are complex and interdependent; every function provides essential services to the rest of the system, often without even realizing it. This is where teamwork comes into play. I like to think about it this way:

Each team in an organization is equally valuable. However, if there's no solid, reciprocal communication between them, they fail to amount to an ideal whole; one plus one plus one equals less than three, so to speak. If you strengthen the connections between the disparate parts, on the other hand, they build upon one another: One plus one plus one equals more than three because each point of addition reinforced the connection between the different components of the equation.

The dangers of silos include much more than basic issues of stalling and miscommunication. If parts of the organization end up moving in different directions at different speeds, you may be running a massive strategic risk. In a siloed organization, you're likely to be running higher operational risk and operational inefficiencies. You may have unidentified key person risk. And if duplicating or compensating behavior is too high, you may end up with reduced productivity and innovation as well as lower morale, possibly resulting in a negative impact on customer service.

This may be easy enough to understand in theory, but it becomes a lot more difficult when it comes to actually identifying silos within your organization.

There are several reasons why silos may not be readily apparent. Sometimes people are compensating for potential issues with manual adjustments. Sometimes they're preoccupied with building their own software. Sometimes they maintain their own Excel spreadsheet outside of the company's main database. The core issue is that blind spots are inevitable. Each team, operating as an individual, likely won't understand the number of interdependencies that they share with the other hardworking teams.

With that in mind, how *can* we go about identifying and remedying silos? There are a number of red flags to keep in mind, including:

- complex organization charts
- redundant/duplicated efforts between teams
- compensating behaviors

- little to no communication preceding a major internal change
- patchwork of internal software
- internal competition between teams

Look for potential silos across functions and geographical regions and consider the increased risk of silos if your team members are operating on a work-from-home basis.

Even once you've identified silos within your organization, figuring out how to actually address them is a whole different can of worms. Since silo-based issues intrinsically involve several moving parts, it's not as though you can identify a single person who's responsible for the problem. With that in mind, what *can* you do?

For starters, establish your goal: You want your teams to have a view of the bigger picture and a concrete understanding of their interdependencies. The best way to achieve this is through improved communication within the individual nodes of your organization. For example, have the engineering or product team sit with someone from the customer service team for a few days in order to better understand interdependencies: How will a change in the software impact the customer service team downstream? Ultimately, you may need to redesign the architecture of some—or even all—of your processes. You may need to delve into the different components of the processes themselves in order to make them more modular.

The fact of the matter is that deconstructing silos will never be an easy task, but it will always be an essential one. You may have to use an iterative trial and error process. Just stay patient, focused, and critical.

OVERCOMING INTERNAL RESISTANCE

I can all but guarantee that one of the biggest obstacles you'll encounter throughout your career will be internal resistance. This often occurs due to the formation of internal silos, but a number of other factors may also apply. Simply enough, people are more inclined to do things the way they're used to and can be afraid of change. But that's not always optimal for the organization.

I've encountered a certain scenario several times across many different firms. While trying to design and implement a large product interest for a key client, an internal stakeholder would prefer to start small and test the waters before trying to fulfill the entire size. While this is an understandable perspective, it becomes complicated when it clashes with the client's needs. The question then becomes: What's really driving the key stakeholder's decisions? And, as I've found to usually be the case: How can we communicate with the stakeholder so that they're willing to get onboard with the larger product order that the client is seeking? It turns out that the answer lies in the routes of internal communication that we utilize. Whenever this happened to me, I discovered that the reason for the stakeholder's reluctance was that they had very little inclusion in the process itself. The key was to increase their participation and awareness of the project's progress. This provided more visibility into the process, creating a sense of ownership that allowed the stakeholder to be far more comfortable engaging in a large-scale transaction.

No matter your situation, if you find yourself facing internal resistance, you need to focus on listening and understanding the drivers for resistance. The vast majority of the time, nobody within your organization is going to be resisting out of sheer stubbornness or malice. People want the company to do well, as an extension of wanting themselves to do well. Instead, you'll find that reluctant parties feel the way that they do due to a fear of change, a problem with internal competition, or a potential consequence to their own well-being, such as the threat of longer working hours. The organization may also have a history of failure when attempts were made to execute similar changes on a large scale.

Once you understand the drivers at work, you can work with people one-on-one to communicate your appreciation for their concerns. Try to get them involved by redesigning incentives, clearly establishing plans for implementation, and breaking down big changes into a series of smaller steps. Let me reiterate: This should be done on a personal, individual basis, not in the midst of a large meeting or committee. In the latter case, people may find themselves uncomfortable and alienated when put on the spot in front of everyone else. When it does come to larger gatherings, work on building a consensus ahead of time via one-on-one conversations. Whenever possible, meetings should be used for the presentation of previously agreed-upon action plans rather than a forum in which to make the decisions themselves.

You may also encounter internal resistance when it comes to new joiners within your organization. This should generally be expected, since they'll be entering with an array of fresh perspectives and different experiences. Think carefully about how to leverage the value of their unique knowledge in face of resistance typically expressed with a *this is how we do things here*-type attitude. Listen to their suggestions with an open mind, encourage new ideas, and offer your help in advocating for them during communications with other teams.

I've often been hired because I offered something new and different that could help develop and grow part of a business. At one firm, I was informed right away that people who don't gel with the culture of the team don't last long. This didn't mean that I shouldn't try to facilitate change; after all, that's what got me hired in the first place. What it did mean was this: If you can fit into the culture, you'll have plenty of room to initiate change without encountering too much resistance as a consequence.

'Culture' is a layered concept with many different definitions. The way I define culture is as a very personal, very subjective thing; it has to do with how an individual prefers to think, communicate, and strategize, almost like a unique language. This can manifest in something as straightforward as a preference for verbal exchanges rather than instant messaging. One salesperson several years ago mentioned that they preferred working with me for exactly this reason: They felt that speaking to one another in person was more efficient, more informative, and more helpful when it came to building strong connections. For other people, the opposite may be true. Neither method of communication is inherently better than the other but learning people's personal preferences is vital to effective leadership. I think of this as learning the personal language of every individual and knowing how to speak with people in a way that aligns with their motivations, fears, abilities, and strategies. 'Culture' also embodies the overall way of doing things and the processes that one will follow in the absence of clear instructions. The right culture is especially key when decisions need to be made under pressure.

This is even more important in multinational or multicultural organizations. For instance, consider the phrase "I'm okay." In English, this is a euphemistic way to communicate that someone's day is going poorly. In French, on the other hand, it means that their day has been genuinely good so far. There isn't always a literal difference of spoken language involved, but the same concept applies to every facet of intra-organizational communication.

DIVERSITY OF THOUGHT

I've been directly involved in campus recruiting for several years, and my strategy is to aim for four team characteristics: high motivation, high ability to collaborate with people, high performance, and high diversity of profiles. The first three are self-explanatory, since I want to build the strongest group possible. What, though, is the value of diversity of thought?

Until college, I participated in an educational system with a strict route of progression: Students were ranked on academic criteria, then selected to participate in competitive exams based upon those criteria. Leadership, soft skills, and the ability to form real human connections with people weren't given much consideration.

When the learning process is structured in this way, everyone who undergoes it will then tend to address problems in the same way. They may have the same blind spots and the same expectations, possibly with less developed interpersonal development and creative potential.

In a nutshell, different profiles and backgrounds strengthen a team by offering different ways of thinking. An international team member, for example, may identify strengths and weaknesses in our current mode of operation by asking something as simple as "Why do we do things in this way?" When prompted to consider these questions, I'll often identify blind spots that I may not have considered at first, where the potential for improvement is high. I can also build strong, synergetic collaboration by designing projects that allow people to work in tandem, and by rotating those projects across different team members, dipping into each of their perspectives to obtain a rich, cohesive final product.

When it comes to high performance, there are more factors in play than one may think. Performance isn't synonymous with "revenue target," but rather refers to the potential to participate in a long-term team in order to create sustainable value for clients and for the organization. Motivation, collaboration, communication, and eagerness to learn are some core characteristics that I'll usually be looking for. Having relevant hard skills is always a plus, but merely possessing the abilities necessary to learn those skills within a reasonable timeline can be equally effective—or even *more* effective, since it opens up an opportunity to ask those aforementioned "Why?" questions.

High performers perceive the primary mission of the organization in a number of different ways, and it's important to identify how their understanding of something may or may not align with the actuality of the matter. Incentives, goals, and metrics may appear differently to different people, and motivations are likely to vary, as well; not everyone is driven primarily by their career or their compensation. To avoid misalignment, my main strategy is to over-communicate. Make sure that *everything* is out in the open, even if it doesn't seem necessary. Ironing out any potential misunderstandings is key to establishing and sustaining a strong team.

LEARNING AND COACHING THROUGH REPETITION

Successful coaching is founded on repetition. This concept is associated more with sports than with academia, but it's absolutely critical to strong leadership and developing people throughout their own journeys.

Athletic coaching tends to be structured around individualized training, lots of repetition, and dedicated workouts to improve a given specific skill.

Academic learning tends to be structured around the expectation that large amounts of information would be processed and retained very quickly, often within a single teaching session, one or two homework sessions, some self-paced reading, and an exam. Everyone receives more or less the same training, little of it is tailored to the individual.

A better alternative is to consider each individual's learning progression independently, similarly to athletic coaching. Pay attention to strengths and weaknesses that you observe among your team members and offer tailored guidance and custom practice opportunities to anyone who could use development in a particular area. Shape the coaching according to the individual's learning curve. Your team is not a monolith, and it shouldn't be treated as such. When you only use one method of performance measurement, some people may seem to fall short; when you examine their abilities from all angles, on the other hand, you may find significant potential for synergetic teamwork. Think about the common saying that's frequently misattributed to Albert Einstein: "Everybody is a genius. But if you judge a fish by its ability to climb a tree, it will live its whole life believing that it is stupid." Einstein himself may never have said such a thing, but that doesn't keep it from being a brilliant little snippet of wisdom.

Training should be a constant flow of repetition and discipline, rather than a single bar to pass, and the team itself should grow comfortable enough with constant changes and new challenges that it will continue to evolve long after your departure. With this in mind, remember that everyone on your team is going to be constantly evolving, including yourself. Your ultimate goal as a team lead should be to make your current self obsolete. In other words, other team members should be able to take over for you in the future so that you're able to pursue new opportunities. This can apply to your high performers, as well; if they find new growth opportunities, they'll likely leave in order to pursue them. Consider this a success! If you anticipate a shift in your team population as time goes on, you'll be able to handle it with ease, and use it as an opportunity to bring in a range of diverse and promising talent that can bring a fresh look to the business.

HUMILITY

I worked hard at my first job. I received strong performance reviews and was therefore under the impression that I was above my current position. My overconfidence led to a number of poor career decisions, and I ended up back where I started.

This wasn't a personal vice of mine. Many, including wonderful people and phenomenal performers, struggle with overconfidence or arrogance at some point in their career. When you let this sort of thing drive you, you may be setting yourself up for disaster. This is what Robin Sharma meant by the words, "Nothing fails like success." Instead, *stay humble*. Admit your mistakes. Give credit where credit is due. When the stars are aligned in your favor, be conscious of and grateful for that fact.

Always check yourself for symptoms of overconfidence and complacency. Many people don't realize that they've grown too comfortable in themselves until it's too late, and they find that they don't know how to respond to an unexpected disruption. Think about your blind spots. Are you acutely aware of the people and outside factors that drive your own success, the success of your team, and the success of your organization? Are your competitors beginning to catch up with you? Are you relying on the same products year after year? Is a key client failing to renew their contract? Did an entire support team that was key to your success just resign?

When these things happen—and they *will*—disruption is the most inevitable thing that there is; remind yourself to adapt. Everyone and everything are in a constant cycle of growth and change, failure and success. Maintain strong relationships and remember to learn the languages of the people and the world around you. Stay humble.

AUTHOR BIO

Vincent Samat is the leader of a product and client solutions team in capital markets in a business-to-business context. His responsibilities include product development and design, product pricing strategy, putting products into production, internal and external product marketing, and occasionally product sales. He has experience at large global American and European firms in financial services, as well as smaller entrepreneurial firms. Vincent has a history of taking on new challenges, especially when it comes to originating and expanding new products and driving significant growth in specific segments. He currently leads a product team with a revenue scope well into nine figures.

Across multiple organizations, he has successfully and consistently performed in high pressure environments with highly competitive people, improved business processes, fostered increased collaboration between teams, revived products for dormant client segments, created innovative products, differentiated positioning versus competitors, proactively driven revenue growth from zero to eight figures at several firms, hired and trained high performers and mentored a number of people at various stages of their careers. He has been selected for a number of programs for his high potential and leadership abilities. Vincent also sits on the board of a non-profit dedicated to improving the life of apparel workers in Haiti.

CHAPTER 3

Leveraging Your Uniqueness

BY RISHAB SHAH

OVER THE YEARS I have crystalized a personal mantra: "Be the person you want them to see." I've echoed this to the executives I advise, to the customers for whom I build products, to my wife, and to my close friends. The wording is deliberate and intended to remind us to connect the greatest aspirations we see for ourselves with the conviction of the daily tactics we must execute to get there.

I've never liked to think of my "professional life" as its own entity. There's something cold and inauthentic about distancing myself from my work in such a way. The version of me that works and the version of me that engages in leisure are one and the same, and always have been. This interconnectedness is something that I see in all successful people. As I've developed my skills and learned more about the world, I've come to identify four key values that have been at the root of all my major accomplishments. By sharing what my experiences have taught me, my goal is not only to provide guidance for those with similar aspirations to my own, but also to distill years' worth of experience into a set of lessons from which anyone can glean insight and helpful lessons.

Getting to this point has not been easy. Success in leadership is often about trial and error—identifying and embracing the areas in which you fail, while simultaneously acknowledging and optimizing those in which you excel. At their core, all my strategies depend on one firm conviction: Anything can be a strength. And I really do mean "anything," whether it be a hobby, a passion, an attitude, an activity, a relationship... The list is infinite. Where followers may try to conform with standards and expectations by excelling in a wide range of abilities, I believe that leaders define themselves through unique assets. They don't try to make themselves into someone they aren't, even if that "someone" seems to be the ideal performer in their particular line of work. It may seem trite, but our differences are what make us strong. It's only through them that we can truly distinguish ourselves from the crowd and deliver the exceptional service that our clients deserve.

Over the duration of my career so far, I've made what I consider to be four major accomplishments. The first and most general is the act of achieving top 10% performance within a large strategy consulting firm. These firms command the premium rates they do because they attract and recruit the top of the talent pool. They then groom these recruits into brilliant business executives through a combination of investing heavily in their long-term development and providing them rapid accelerated exposure across a large surface area of industry clients. Carving out a space for myself amongst this esteemed group is valuable to me because of the way that it speaks to the efficacy of my personal strategies. People who can reliably and productively do their jobs are crucial to the function of business and society at large. And I have colleagues that can easily take on tasks that completely stump me. By distinguishing myself through my unique strengths, however, I've found how I can be the best and most effective version of myself.

My flagship engagement within the firm involved a nationally televised scandal with a very material human impact; picture cameras outside, monitoring our activity daily. I would use the industry skills and business judgement that I then gained to launch a venture fund and help grow four separate startups within the unprecedented constraints of the COVID-19 pandemic. Now, I'm in the midst of building new software products for a massive digital health startup.

I'm not listing out my accomplishments to boast. Quite to the contrary, I hope to emphasize how things like this are imminently achievable, no matter where you start off. Furthermore, they all involve a theme of earnest personal and professional growth and discipline. I was able to do these things because I believed in them, and in my ability to make them happen. It is my hope that I can help you to feel the same way about your own greatest goals.

TRANSFERABILITY OF SKILLS

I founded my first micro-startup out of my college dorm room and sold it when I started grad school. It wasn't a huge exit event, but it did gift me two valuable lessons. Firstly, I gained an understanding of the boiled-down fundamentals for how any business actually operates –

minus all the business journal level philosophizing. Secondly, it taught me a deep and lasting lesson in empathy for executives, founders, and other business owners who have their personal reputation and livelihood on the line.

From micro, I went macro – so I eventually joined the largest corporate strategy practice in the US. From the start, I learned quickly, and strived to consistently deliver high-quality work. I attribute this high performance to a specific strategy that I learned to utilize: Rather than just participating in certain systems, my goal was to discern how they worked–and, more importantly, *why* they worked the way that they did. Tracking the actions and instincts of my superiors, I found myself questioning why certain engagements were scoped the way that they were. Why, for instance, did CEOs move beyond mere transaction during their sales proposals? What other goals were they working to attain by discussing seemingly unrelated long-term implications of clients' businesses and lives?

At the time, I was working Saturdays and Sundays, and I couldn't help but notice that several partners were also coming in on the weekends. Why was that? After all, it wasn't as if they could be interacting with clients, which I assumed to be the foundation of all the work that they did. It was through close observation that I came to realize that the term "sales proposal" was in itself something of a misnomer. "Proposal" was less accurate than "communication," and true communication necessitates equal interest between its participants. The process wasn't so much about transactionality as it was about relationship building–about coaching clients into an understanding of where they wanted to go not only with their businesses, but with their lives as a whole.

One particular partner took a special interest in me. Since I came to see her so often, she began to recognize the ways in which I might be of value to her: I was "closer to the ground," so to speak, and therefore had access to particular perspectives that she may have more trouble understanding. She began to ask me my opinions on her cases—questions to which I, of course, always provided frank answers. Through exchanges like this, we were able to build up a lot of trust, to the point where she trusted me to communicate directly to the client. This sort of "snowball effect" continued to build, enabling me to take on larger and larger duties. I dedicated increasing amounts of time to making notes and writing up specific points to address with the clients.

After six months, I had sold over a million dollars' worth of work, an achievement typically reserved for partners who were several levels above me at the time. I give credit for this success to a simple philosophy by which I consistently abided: In order to succeed, you need to invest in transferable skills.

Transferability of skills comes from having the proper mindset. Wherever you are right now—whether it be school, a consulting job, a career in an entirely different industry, or even no career at all—you can use the lessons that you're being taught. Your current environment, whatever it may be, contains elements that can and will aid you in your future goals.

The key to implementing this forward-thinking mindset is to establish a rough image of where you want to be in the future. At what point will you consider yourself successful? I like to refer to this goal post as a "golden bullet"—one valuable standout point that will shape all of your other actions. I recommend all my direct reports, before even starting their new role, internship, project, or leadership position, to write that "golden bullet" onto their resume. Then at the start of every day, I ask them to work backwards from the golden bullet and focus on what useful skills you can glean from your current occupation to make it come true. This is the same technique that I also like to use while building relationships with clients. My goal with my executive clients is to get a sense of their biggest goal, both in their businesses and in their personal lives. Then I work to find ways to solve their current, smaller problems in a way that will be ultimately beneficial in the client's larger personal journey. Not every step you take can instantly lead to achieving your dreams, but that doesn't mean you can't be walking in the right direction.

One of the most important things to do is to keep yourself away from a "bench warming" mindset. Many people look at their less exciting experiences as necessary evils, to be completed as quickly as possible and then left in the dust. "I'll just knock out a couple of years at an investment bank," you might find yourself thinking, "and then start working towards what I actually want to achieve." This type of thinking can be incredibly harmful to your prospects. You should never frame an opportunity as just "getting things out of the way." No matter where you are, there's always *something* to learn.

Another way to look at this is to think of yourself like a machine learning (ML) model. From the very beginning, a piece of ML is programmed to know its ultimate objective. Whenever it receives data, it parses through every point, slowly pulling out anything that it finds helpful. Then, through gradual assembly of all these disparate bits of information, it becomes able to construct the tools necessary for achieving that primary objective. Just like the AI in this metaphor, you should always know your golden bullet—your objective function. If you lose track of it, you're going to miss out on obtaining valuable information and perspectives. And if that happens, you truly will be wasting your time.

Arguably, we have entered a period where most of the professional workforce have access to largely the same information. Therefore, the new competitive advantage is how effectively one can combine these facts into unique and meaningful points of view. Bonus points if it's not obvious. This way, you can organize the business to optimize for this point of view quickly, creating a difficult to replicate economic moat. From that point, your focus becomes how effectively you can generate a strategy and actionable roadmap based on that point of view. Finally, it's about how effectively you can organize the right existing resources and people to execute that roadmap and strategy.

This nonlinear convergence of skills is what enabled me to perform duties that largely exceeded any expectations people may have had for my role at the time. By being able to jump between different areas, we can distinguish ourselves as highly effective leaders who are capable of taking on manifold responsibilities. When you can make use of the accumulation of skills gained throughout your entire career, your potential value will increase exponentially.

The moral of the story? It doesn't matter where you are now, so long as you know where you want to go. If your current situation doesn't align with your career goals, you don't need to shift that situation; you only need to change how you approach it. When you use your present environment to compound relevant skills and information, you'll be moving yourself up the ladder to success, even when that progress isn't visible at the moment.

LEANING INTO UNIQUENESS

Throughout my career, I've always found myself subconsciously operating under the baseline assumption that everyone around me is doing some version of the "right" thing. I wouldn't go so far as to call this a case of imposter syndrome; it could more accurately be described as an acute awareness of my own individuality, and how it operates in conjunction with the behavior of others. My instinct tells me that, if I'm doing something differently from the crowd, I must be making some mistake, or violating some unspoken rule. This has led me to attempt to standardize myself to the norm when it comes to mannerisms, image, and more. Feeling this way is more common than people may realize, but the truth is that our unique assets are exactly what make us valuable.

Of course, you should still make an effort to learn from those around you. Observing your coworkers and the way that they speak, dress, and converse is a great way to understand and adapt to the culture of your workplace. At the same time, this approach has a certain level of diminishing returns. The more you standardize, the fewer opportunities you'll have to take advantage of what makes you uniquely valuable.

What do I mean by "uniquely valuable?" Well, that depends on you. Think about it this way: There is *something* at which you particularly excel. If you can organize your career to better align with that "something," you'll establish a defense against the natural biology of boredom and burnout. On your absolute lowest day, your unique "something" requires so little effort that you can still perform it at a level comparable to most other people. This gives you an inherent competitive advantage, and if you can figure out how to optimize it, you'll find yourself excelling instead of simply succeeding.

For me personally, my unique value lies in my love of reading. Even if I'm sick in bed and unable to do an ounce of work, I'm still going to be reading books, newspapers, and anything else that I can get my hands on. Because of this, I'm naturally able to augment any discussion with a wide range of ideas taken from seemingly irrelevant subject matter. I'm always passively obtaining information, and I'm constantly on the lookout for opportunities to converge that information in a helpful way. Since I know this to be my primary unique asset, I try to organize my firm around opportunities to take advantage of it. I don't need to be the best at everything, or even at most things–but if I'm the best at one thing, and if I can structure my work in such a way that I'm constantly drawing upon that one thing, it's just as effective.

Many workplaces push the saccharine and ultimately hollow narrative of everyone being different and contributing their own strengths to their jobs, resulting in a lively and diverse workplace. While that's a nice enough sentiment, it doesn't do much to help you move forward in the business world. Just *knowing* that I like to read wouldn't automatically give me any sort of competitive advantage. The much more important part is my ability to construct systems around me that allow me to utilize my love of reading in as many areas of my work as possible.

The key to building these systems has to do with how you frame and market yourself and your business. For instance, I run a boutique firm. One system that I've adopted involves the email messages that I frequently send regarding the business. Within these messages, I include a deliberate–but not overbearing–degree of repetition when it comes to specific topics, including the market entry and construction of competitive advantage. My recipients then come to subconsciously position me as someone who works particularly well in those areas—so that, if they do reach out to me, I don't need to worry about optimizing my unique asset, because I've already framed myself in that way.

Of course, there's a flip side to this approach: When you direct the majority of your energy towards optimizing your unique asset, you may fall short in other areas. You shouldn't completely neglect any skill set, of course, but you also need to be able to recognize when you aren't the best person for a particular job. This is when your personal team and network of coworkers becomes important. In addition to recognizing what makes you special, try to surround yourself with people who possess complementary qualities. Think of it like building a superhero team. If you have the gift of super strength and nothing else, you'll be able to save the day in many situations—in others, however, you're only as effective as any old civilian. If the power of invisibility, flight, super-speed, or shape-shifting is needed in order to bring down the latest bad guy, you're in rough shape... unless you have a team built up around you, full of heroes with unique assets. The more diverse your network is, the more situations you'll be able to effectively tackle.

To bring this back to the real world, think about it from the client's perspective. It's wonderful to have the reassurance that you're working with someone who specializes in a particular area, but it's even better if that person can give you access to other people with different areas of expertise. Your team is far more effective if each of you is incredible at one thing than if all of you are decent at everything.

This also means that you'll find yourself needing to delegate work to others when you feel that you won't be able to do the best possible job with it. Don't let this discourage you. Teamwork is never a weakness—in fact, being able to recognize when you aren't the best person for a task is absolutely integral to being an effective leader. It's all about juggling your options to give your client the best experience possible.

As a product leader, I think being different is also about being critical about when and what to emulate. For instance, I often see product managers (PMs) perfunctorily following certain industry artifacts or frameworks. There is nothing wrong with re-using best practice - but when pressed upon why - their rationale is based on "X does it this way - and clearly, they have released successful products." The "X" is whichever Silicon Valley heavyweight company you choose to insert. The challenge is that we tend to over-venerate these companies without understanding the underlying organization and conditions which make their practices or frameworks successful. Hypothetically, maybe Apple prioritizes detailed customer personas as the basis of their design process. They may minimize another common framework in PM called "jobs to be done," which focuses on what tasks you can eliminate or simplify for your customer. At an earlier start-up stage, this may lead a PM to say that their team must also invest considerable time in creating and maintaining detailed customer personas documentation. But if you take a step back, maybe this works for Apple because it has very senior PMs and designers who have seasoned experience translating customer personas into actionable products. Maybe Apple's product SKUs are more mature, and targeting personas allows them to expand and identify more niche customer groups for their existing products. Perhaps Apple has invested significant marketing resources to position themselves as category creators, so their customers expect new workflows rather than making current tasks more efficient. The PM at the earlier stage company likely has a mismatch on all three counts. Her junior PMs cannot translate the personas, are trying to launch their first product without any previous mature SKUs, and have a limited marketing budget. The early-stage PM is quickly frustrated when this supposed marquee tool is not getting the desired results. At best, they abandon it—and some time and effort have been wasted. At worst—they double down and sink more resources and time into a mismatched strategy.

The lesson here is to take the time to understand *why* specific tactics work for others and lean into knowing underlying characteristics that make you unique and let that guide how you lead and what you choose to emulate.

BEING OBSESSIVE AND CURIOUS

Even as I've shaped my career around my unique capabilities, I've still had days where my interest in my work wanes. This is more than just normal; it's completely human. Contemporary ideals of efficiency tend to treat workers like robots, assuming that everyone has the potential to operate only within the constraints of their bodily needs, rather than their mental and emotional ones. But, as far as companies may try to press this narrative, it's simply untrue. Everyone ends up being a victim of complacency and boredom at some point. Rather than trying to avoid this, the best thing you can do is acknowledge it and find ways to minimize it whenever possible.

I've found one particular strategy that works for me in this way. If I had to describe my attitude in approaching tedious work in a single word, it would be *obsessive*.

Now, "obsessive" has some negative connotations. Let me clear up some of the things that I'm *not* talking about. I don't mean that you should prioritize one part of a project to the point of neglecting others. I don't mean that you should be a perfectionist who doesn't know how to compromise. And I certainly don't mean that you should let your work completely consume your life. As a matter of fact, I'm speaking more along the lines of the opposite: You should make every effort to let your *life* consume your *work*.

The way to do this is by reframing every task that you take on. Take a moment to engage in some self-reflection and find something–anything–that you know you love unconditionally. What overarching theme in your professional life makes you obsessive? What, regardless of circumstances, will you always enjoy learning and doing? For me, that thing is creation–more specifically, the creation and release of new products. I find nothing in life more fulfilling than the knowledge that I'm putting something new into the world that didn't exist before.

Of course, it isn't realistically feasible for my work to *only* revolve around product creation. The fact of the matter is that I need to engage in a thousand tiny, less interesting tasks in order to attain that one moment of reward. The trick is to approach them through the lens of my obsession. If I frame all of my work in terms of how it contributes to my ultimate goal, I can find some degree of fulfillment in even the most mundane of assignments.

Here's an example of what I mean. Some days, I'll take a look at my calendar for the next week, and I'll be greeted by a whole array of frankly unexciting meetings. Many people will give a sigh, buckle down, and resign themselves to another round of boring engagements, none of which feel genuinely important to the achievement of their goals. What I do is a little different. I look at each and every meeting as an opportunity to make progress towards the thing that I've identified as an obsession. What do they each contribute towards the act of putting something new in the world? And, if the answer seems to be "nothing," what can I do to change that? For instance, a marketing meeting could be an opportunity for product promotion. If I help more people learn about a product, that will inch it closer to success, even by the tiniest of margins. In making that my focus, I'm able to approach the meeting in a new light. Does this reframing automatically make it the most thrilling thing in the world? Of course not. But it does make a difference, and sometimes that difference is all you need.

There's one more key ingredient at work here: deliberate intention. Perhaps, as you just now read the word "obsessive," you were reminded of trite company principles—the type that you'd find painted in too-cheery, rainbow-colored letters across the wall of a break room. The notions of obsessiveness and curiosity are far too often employed in a disingenuous manner—or, at the very least, a dispassionate one. The problem with this is that curiosity cannot be forced, period. If you try to do so, you'll only end up more frustrated than ever, stuck with the fact that even your so-called "obsession" has left you hopelessly jaded. You can't *create* an obsession—you have to find one that already exists. This means that you need to be honest with yourself. What are you naturally drawn towards? Be *deliberate* in identifying your obsessive lens. Don't try to make yourself curious about anything and everything, because the simple truth of the matter is that you won't be.

CLEAR AND STRUCTURED THINKING

I've never considered myself to be a great salesman. Identifying and embracing my weaknesses is what enables me to do the same with my strengths, and to find a balance between them that pushes me to perform at my maximum personal potential. All of us have some areas in which we may not excel, and there's no reason to let that hold us back.

So, even if I'm not a naturally gifted salesman, I can nonetheless acknowledge that I've always been a believer in the importance of good listening skills. I'm an empathetic person who knows how to process and respond to clients' problems with their own wants and needs in mind. The best way to use that empathy, I've found, is to structure clients' feelings, problems, or anxieties in a way that can be executed upon.

Structured, clear thinking is a huge part of my professional process, without which I would never be in the leadership position that I am today. Simply speaking: Without proper structure, clear communication cannot exist.

Though many people will tell you otherwise, communication isn't just about the way that you package a message. It's also about how you frame that message in your own mind, and how you can work closely with someone in order to organize their vision for execution.

A lot of people—including me, you, and any client that either of us will ever work with—will often feel a lot of self-doubt when it comes to taking on obligations and responsibilities. As in the case of the professional *ennui* that I previously discussed, you have nothing to gain by trying to deny the existence of this self-doubt. Once you accept it, you can work on finding an effective antidote. For me, that antidote is the act of structuring.

When you learn how to properly structure a client's vision, it will naturally combat the self-doubt that you feel. Let me explain what I mean in a little bit more depth: Doubt of any sort has its roots in the unknown. When you enter an engagement without knowing how you're going to communicate, you'll be operating at a subpar level of confidence before you've even properly gotten started. But when you have a structured plan, you know your answer to every possibility. You close out potential loopholes, thereby eliminating the threat of the unknown and bolstering your confidence as well as that of your client.

Not too long ago, I engaged in a peculiar nightly ritual. As soon as all of my social and professional obligations for the day were complete, I would sit by myself and try to anticipate every single conversation that might occur the next day. I don't just mean business conversations, either; if I expected to run into an old friend or call up a family member, that would go on the list. And at that point, it was a literal, physical list: I would write these thoughts down on paper.

As tedious as the process was, it made a world of difference when it came to combatting my anxieties. For each conversation, I wrote what was essentially a miniature essay, encapsulating any point that either side might make. I identified every possible outcome and processed my thoughts concerning it. After nights upon nights of taking the time to write these things down, thinking in this pattern became second nature. The content generated was never the goal – instead performing this in real-time allowed for effortless and productive interactions.

When you need to increase your own confidence and encourage

other people to believe in you, this tree-like structure of potentiality is an exceptionally powerful tool to alleviate self-doubt. Here's what one of these visualizations of possibility might look like on any given night:

I know that I might run into a particular client the next day. If this happens, the client is going to have one main question for me: Should we or should we not enter a new market? There are two overarching responses to this: yes and no. I'll write these down, then spend a little time with each of them, examining their implications. If the answer that I give is "yes," what reasons do I have to cite? How will the client respond, and what will be the ultimate result of our exchange? I'll then do the same for the "no" option, then trace each option to its natural conclusion, making a note of every point at which a new sub-question may emerge.

Of course, I won't be able to break down every possible path that the conversation could take—without getting into the thick of the mathematics, suffice to say that trying to do so would spiral out of control very quickly. Instead, I make use of intuition to choose the points and paths of conversation that feel the most naturally compelling. If I hit a dead end, at which the conversation feels as though it can reach no productive outcome, I'll backtrack, identify the decision that brought me to this end, and eliminate it as an option.

By the time I've worked through all of the realistic routes of the interaction in this manner, I'll be tremendously more confident during the conversation itself. Whenever I make a proposal, suggestion, or decision, I'll have an implicit understanding and internal reference as to why my ideas are legitimate. Sure, the client may not get all the way down to the weeds of the matter—in fact, they shouldn't; that's my job, not theirs. But I can rest assured that, no matter in which direction they choose to press me, I'll be able to back up my answers with clearly reasoned thinking.

While I've described this strategy in the context of a business exchange, I'd like to once again reiterate the fact that it can and should be applied to much more than that. If you internalize structured thinking as a strategy to use in your private and personal matters as well as your public and professional ones, it will become far more natural and therefore more effective.

Merging these two sides of yourself is a good practice in general, too. If you try to go about your life switching in and out of "business mode," you'll find it to be unnatural and stressful. The strengths of your professional life can aid you in your personal life, and vice versa. To be an effective leader, you need to allow yourself to be a complete human being, not just a partner or employee.

FACING RESISTANCE

All of us often have moments in our lives and careers where we want to achieve something big, bold, and ambitious. Even if we are completely convinced of our own ability to do whatever this critical "something" may be, it can feel like an uphill battle when it comes to convincing other people to believe in us. This becomes a problem when those other people possess the power or resources that we need in order to achieve our vision. We may be positive that we could prove ourselves if given the opportunity–but the issue lies in whether we'll be able to obtain that opportunity in the first place.

There are only really two ways to respond in this situation that will consistently give the results that we're looking for. Simply continuing to push against someone else's resistance isn't one of them. When you're convinced of your own position, it can be tempting to try employing logic, with the thought that *surely* your opposition will be able to see the light when given enough information. This attitude is ineffective because it leads you to deny the existence of the internal biases of both parties—your own as well as the stakeholder's. The harder you push, the more strain you're going to put on your relationship. It's basically the equivalent of holding a conversation in which the other person is clearly just waiting for you to stop talking so that they can say their own piece. If someone has made it clear that they aren't going to budge, you need to be able to recognize when to back down.

Backing down, however, isn't the same as giving up. All it means is that you need to take an alternate approach. In my experience, there are a couple of ways to go about this, depending on the context of the situation.

Your first option is to prioritize their goals over yours. When you have opposing ideas about how to go about attacking a problem or project, it's only natural that the other party will resist "giving in" to your perspective—and the more you try to convince them, the more stubborn they're bound to become. This is because you're creating an environment of opposition, in which they feel like they need to fight to prove the integrity of their own vision. You can avoid this by acknowledging the importance of what they're trying to achieve. Use your energy and ingenuity to find unique and effective results for their vision instead of solely focusing on your own. This builds a powerful foundation of trust rooted in genuine intention of trying to help the other person, and you will be better positioned to get this person's support in the future, once the time comes to go about pursuing your own goals and ideas.

The act of putting your vision aside in the short-term leans into natural human reciprocity, which is an extremely valuable concept to utilize in your life and career. Leadership isn't about always being in the right, but rather about learning how to craft mutually beneficial solutions to what may initially seem to be a conflict of interests. A good leader knows that every perspective within a team holds value.

Still, there are times when the technique of putting your needs second won't be ideal. Sacrificing your vision in the short term isn't always going to be an option, or the right step to take. Maybe your idea is too important, maybe time is a factor, or maybe it just doesn't feel intuitively right to put your goals on the back burner. All of these are legitimate reasons to try a different strategy. Remember that the merits of your ideas will never be enough to convince someone who doesn't want to be convinced. Your job then becomes finding someone who *does* want to be convinced, so that you can move forward in your work. In other words, you'll need to change your environment.

I have no small amount of first-hand experience trying to work through problems like this. For a long time, I tried to pitch an ambitious new venture program to a past employer. I approached a senior executive armed with hard data. We had capital, we had a workforce, we had visibility—we had, in short, every possible reason on paper to engage in the venture capital business. If I do say so myself, I was very convincing—and yet my ability to argue my point wasn't the issue so much as the fact that I had to argue it in the first place. The senior executive had a different vision of what they wanted to do with the practice. When I offered an alternative, I was implicitly disparaging the value of that vision and disregarding all of the thought and hard work that they had put into it. Nobody likes feeling dismissed. Persuading a person to change their mind isn't the same as solving a logic puzzle, because we're all naturally determined to stick to our own passions and convictions. Effective leaders know this and use it to their advantage in order to optimize the efficiency of their visions' execution.

In another context, I may have chosen to back down and put the senior executive's goals before mine, in order to make use of that aforementioned natural human reciprocity. However, I was operating under extenuating circumstances that limited the viability of this option: We were in the midst of the global COVID-19 pandemic. I knew that if I were to employ my ideas as soon as possible, they would have valuable results on our struggling society. If I truly wanted to make a difference, I couldn't afford to wait.

So I chose to take my energy elsewhere. I brought my ideas outside of the company, and worked to find someone whose energy and intentions matched my own. Doing this allowed me to launch a successful venture fund with significant benefits for four separate businesses, including a medical transportation company. Throughout my career, nothing has been more fulfilling than the knowledge that I was able to contribute to the medical field in its most dire time of need. I never could have done such a thing without acknowledging that I needed a different environment in which to execute my vision.

In summary: When you find firm resistance, don't feel the need to push. You alone know the value of whatever ambitious idea you hope to pursue. Consider the time and the place, and think about which one needs to be changed in order to get the results that you need. Stay flexible, stay smart, and stay determined, and you'll find that you're able to accomplish just about anything when you set your mind to it.

FINAL TAKEAWAYS

What makes you different? If nothing else, I want you to ask yourself that question. Too many promising people will waste time trying to conform, merely because they don't see themselves as anything more than average or standard. The truth is that there is no such thing as "average;" everyone has their own unique strength, and their success depends on their ability to leverage it.

We're taught to be as "normal" as possible, and to downplay our personal quirks and passions. Moving outside of the constraints of expectation, especially when you're waist-deep in the professional world, can be intimidating. When faced with this mental block, I make an effort to reshape my mindset and start thinking of myself as a product instead of a person.

This might feel counterintuitive. Of course, people are more complex and valuable than products, which are only made to perform some specific function, but the key point is that products are *specialized.* No single object tries to do everything, and it's because of this that they're able to serve their unique purposes so effectively. People are the same way, even if we don't often recognize it. We do our best when we can work together and complement one another's strengths and abilities.

I recently came to learn the acronym "GYLIO," which stands for "get your life in order." A common piece of advice from many self-improvement gurus is that you should take the occasional GYLIO day, during which you set aside all professional obligations and focus solely on changing yourself and your habits in order to lead a more productive lifestyle. While that may work for some people, I'd like to propose an alternate approach based upon the notion that "in order" looks different for different people. You don't need to reshape yourself into something that is more objectively acceptable as an example of success in your field of work. Instead of splitting yourself even more down the middle between the personal and the professional, seek to eliminate the friction between those two halves. You're immensely more valuable as a well-rounded human than you possibly could be as a worker whose only goal is robotic efficiency.

With this in mind, I would like to leave you with one last thought. Take the time to discover your personal market fit. Every product has a place where it will sell the best, because it lines up with a need possessed by a particular populace. Likewise, there is a place in the world where you'll be able to do your best, most important, and most personally fulfilling work. When you are able to work with the people, places, and opportunities that are in need of your unique abilities, you're proving yourself to be someone invaluable and irreplaceable. Be the person you want them to see.

AUTHOR BIO

Rishab Shah is a product leader, management consultant, and venture capitalist. He runs a next-generation advisory firm helping large corporations and earlier-stage companies develop superior digital products and services. Under his guidance, companies and executives realize their full potential by staying relevant, growing their existing business, and generating new revenue streams.

As a product leader, Rishab specializes in the early stages of taking products from idea to first market. He develops SaaS products at a health-tech unicorn start-up valued at $4 billion, using artificial intelligence to reduce the administrative burden for patients and medical practices. He serves as the strategy director of a non-profit that conducts validation trials to determine the impact of new digital health solutions.

Previously, he served executive clients in the healthcare and technology industries, and the government sector for the world's largest consulting firm. His leadership resulted in the generation of over $100 million in value. He also co-founded a venture fund to help portfolio companies build digital products that not only had a positive effect on thousands of lives, but raised millions in funding.

Rishab has spoken at major conferences around the world on new venture models, investment theses, practical leadership, corporate strategy, and building differentiated products. Rishab is based in Georgetown, Washington D.C. with his wife and twin sons. He is a fervent fan of tennis, travel, and coffee shops.

Connect With Rishab: Please feel free to contact him at rishabshah.com if you have any questions or comments.

CHAPTER 4

Freedom From the Crowd

BY RICHMOND WONG

THIS CHAPTER IS FOR entrepreneurs, senior leaders of tech companies, and those in professional services (consulting, law, finance, and accounting) to accomplish more on their own terms. In doing so, you can live lives of the greatest personal and professional freedom using self-leadership concepts that perhaps are quite different from ones you've encountered before. By reading this chapter, you will learn how to live a business and personal life full of productivity, achievement, enjoyment, and freedom according to your own standards—not ones set by others.

More specifically, we'll be discussing the concept of leadership over your own mind and how not to mindlessly follow the dictates of ideas you've assimilated via osmosis that may not be that appropriate for you as an individual and businessperson.

I'm sure you've read many typical leadership books that recommend actions such as setting KPIs, conducting regular strategic reviews, developing your teams, and keeping your office door open.

All of these are completely valid, but what has always bugged me about these types of mass market business titles is that they almost always seem to just skim the surface of leadership by superficially focusing on mere action. What these books fail to achieve is to go one necessary level deeper by giving you insight on how leaders should think and be.

As you know, merely mimicking action without an understanding of the psychology of self-leadership is no recipe for long-term sustained success—particularly as your life and business becomes more complicated.

What I will instead share with you in the following pages is a general mental framework that has driven specific, sustained, and directed action to create and surface ongoing opportunities in all areas of my life.

The components of the mindset are:

1. Permanently free yourself from the 'wisdom' of the crowd
2. Bring what feels impossible into reality by creating it
3. Never again be held hostage by make-or-break situations by increasing your options
4. Consistently beat your competition by leaning into your killer instinct
5. For true control over your future, fine-tune your life stages
6. Discover how to live congruently with yourself using principles and purpose

These mindsets have allowed me to conduct myself in my internal and external worlds (including with clients, peers, and subordinates) so that I have found success in different competitive industries (journalism, law, and tech) in both North America and Asia.

As background, I got my start in journalism at one of Canada's largest media companies, then moved to practicing corporate law at one of the world's 10 largest law firms in their Hong Kong and Shanghai offices. I then became a tech manager at several multinational B2B software firms, running teams and overlooking key projects in developed and emerging markets across Asia before joining the start-up world back in North America.

I've since transitioned to running my own consulting business: this time counseling start-up founders from around the world, along with their senior executives, in both the software and hardware spaces on their highest ROI growth and product management initiatives.

Feel free to adopt some or all of the ideas I present in this chapter. I encourage you to try what works for you while discarding what doesn't. One of the main takeaways from this chapter is personal choice; that is, you choose how you want to best live your life for yourself and for those most important to you—whether they are from your personal or work life.

If you follow all or some of these ideas I share, you can expect to:

- Be more productive and motivated
- Make more money
- Generate challenging new opportunities that meaningfully enhance your business and personal life
- Become more preeminent and distinctive in your niche
- Live a business and personal life in ways that are most congruent with your important personal values.

My hope is that you will find value in these mindsets and that they will benefit your life in the same ways that they have greatly enriched mine.

Ultimately, the end result you will achieve is a new way of thinking, being, and doing to help you live a life that is not a compromise between freedom, enjoyment, innovation, and accomplishment. Put simply, by unnailing your foot from the floor, you'll have much more freedom to maneuver in your thoughts, actions, and plans for the present and future.

Wherever you are in the world and in your life right now, my sincere hope is that these self-leadership concepts will positively transform the way you lead yourself and along with it, everyone you touch.

FREE YOURSELF FROM THE 'WISDOM' OF THE CROWD

Most people live in a box. Every day they go about their professional and personal lives in ways that have already been chosen for them by external ideas and dictates from those still alive, barely alive, or long dead.

These ideas come from a variety of seen and unseen sources: our parents, friends and colleagues, our culture or schooling. It also includes experts, the media and society at large. Because of this, we by default spend most of our waking hours operating on autopilot. Some of these ideas positively influence our lives while others needlessly inhibit our personal development as leaders in our professional and personal lives, causing us to stagnate. Others are even more dangerous because they actively harm us.

Breaking out of this invisible box is important because you as an entrepreneur, senior executive, or professional, will at some point need to make difficult decisions that are in the best interests of yourself, those closest to you, and your business (and the people within it).

In this section, I offer a way of thinking and operating that gives you the possibility of living your personal and business life free (or as free as possible) from the expectations and constraints imposed by the spoken and unspoken expectations of your surroundings and individual history.

In this way, I am defining "breaking out of the box" beyond what is commonly and stereotypically thought of as innovation and creativity. Instead, what I want to introduce to you is a way of operating in the world that maximizes your decision-making latitude and vastly increases the number of options available to you in a rapidly moving, transforming, and competitive world that is only speeding up, not slowing down.

This section of this chapter guides you through the initial step of living a life that most precisely reflects your truest values by first helping you realize just how much of our thoughts and beliefs are not really ours to begin with.

Then for the remainder of this chapter, we will delve into ways to build your own unique life via a set of mindsets, planning tools, and ways of operating in the physical world that will allow you to live in ways that are most congruent with your truest values.

So, to begin, what keeps us trapped is that deep down you (like everyone else) have a need to feel safe, to be right ("I told you so"), and to be liked (approval seeking). All three of these unnecessarily restrict us to dogmatic ways of thinking and acting.

For example, this could include the emotional rush you get when your family shows off your high-status job to relatives which causes you to stick with it despite it not being a good fit for you. It could be you insisting that colleagues in your new job do a project a certain fixed way because it's "supposed to be done that way." Or you stay in a bad relationship since "good people are supposed to tough it out" even when things aren't working and because you're afraid you won't find someone more suitable.

As you can see, this is an incredibly dangerous way to sleepwalk through life and to spend a lifetime living on terms not our own.

However, just being aware of the fact that many of your long-held assumptions and beliefs are neither yours nor to your long-term benefit, means you open yourself to the possibility of living more freely because it will allow you to break through and consciously sculpt your life.

Next, realize you have the ability to control what goes on in your head, meaning you yourself are ultimately responsible for generating, managing, and policing your thoughts. This means that once you're aware of externally induced thoughts influencing your mind, you alone are responsible for deciding whether or not you want to break out of your box. It's not a question of whether you can break through (you can), but a question of whether you want to.

In other words, being able to see ahead down the road will allow you to preemptively avoid the metaphorical potholes in our life. With awareness and newfound sight, you can make the conscious choice to navigate so that you avoid any obstructions that would damage or slow you down.

Of course, living outside the box also means that none of your ways of thinking and acting should cause you to do anything that is illegal or harms others. In other words, living free from the expectations of your surroundings does not mean you have an unconditional and unrestrained pass to act in ways that violate your society's laws or tramples on the rights, security, and safety of others.

Beyond that, however, there is plenty of flexibility in how you conduct yourself so that you can live a life most compatible with your principles and purpose (which we'll discuss in this chapter's final section).

Another compelling reason to break out of the box is not simply because it is a quality of life issue, but because, quite pragmatically, it is a competitive advantage for your business life.

Thinking and acting the same as everybody else confers no competitive differentiation. The reason clients and customers choose their product and service providers is because these providers offer something that is different and better to the buyer that nobody (or few others) can.

If you have trouble freeing yourself from your ingrained patterns of automatic thinking, I encourage you to really think about the ultimate costs you are imposing on yourself at this very moment.

More specifically, each of us only has a limited time on this planet and every moment that has passed is lost forever. We can always find another job if we lose our current one. We can make more money if we lose what we have, and we can recover our health from illness (barring the most serious ones), but we can never get back lost time. This is as true for billionaires as it is for paupers.

Therefore, why would you waste your life living in a way that is not congruent with your most closely held values, beliefs, and ambitions?

I'll use my own life as an example. Most ex-lawyers transition either into legal recruiting or legal editing when they leave the law. (Out of the four traditional professional service segments of finance, consulting, accounting, and law, the last one by far has the narrowest exit opportunities.) However, I wanted something that could better take advantage of my skills in management, operations, and marketing as well as my interest in software. Of course, I had people in my circle tell me that I should stay in legal-related roles because that was "how things worked."

I've always had an independent streak, so I ignored them.

Even though at the time I hadn't formalized the mental frameworks I describe in this chapter, I let my predilection for independent thinking guide me. I knew I didn't have to do what everyone else had done in the past or what those around me opined was in my best interests. Put simply, I didn't need to follow past precedent, nor did I have to submit to societal presumption of what ex-lawyers could do.

Eventually, persisting with what I knew suited me best over the long-term led me to working at multinational tech firms and start-ups, which then led me to my current role advising international start-up founders and senior executives.

Meanwhile, the vast majority of my law school classmates remain lawyers because they are trapped by dogma (e.g., they don't want to disappoint their parents, or they are afraid of how their social circle will judge them if they no longer have the perceived prestige of being a lawyer.) Yet, they hate their jobs—to the detriment of their own lives and of those closest to them in the form of bottled up resentment and regret.

Another way to push yourself out of the box is to think about the ultimate price of inaction (or insufficient action) that you will pay in your business and personal life. For example, if you continue to think and act as you currently do, what will your life look like one year from now? How about two years? Five years?

In addition, what business opportunities will you have missed out on?

What are the fulfilling relationships you could have had? Who could you have been?

While it won't be possible for you to know exactly where you will be in the future, you will almost certainly be able to imagine the negative consequences of your unwillingness to change—including the impact on your personal and professional relationships.

Of course, when I say this, I also acknowledge the reality of your skills and abilities and the possession or non-possession of particular talents will allow you (or not) to live in ways that are congruent with you. For example, someone who wants to become a full-time artist likely will have trouble succeeding in a reasonable timeframe if they don't already have the requisite skills. Conversely, someone who has been coding as a hobbyist since age 12, likely has a very good chance of transitioning to becoming a professional software developer.

At the same time, however, remember that you have agency to create the future you want. You already have certain skills, talents, and relationships to set yourself up for the opportunities that best benefit you. You also have the wherewithal to develop new required skills, talents, and relationships if you don't have them already. The next sections will help you best capitalize on your existing assets, as well as help you develop ones you need.

BRING WHAT FEELS IMPOSSIBLE INTO REALITY

Now that you've broken out of the box, the next step is to create your own reality so that you can not only think the way you want to think, but actually live, work, and have the relationships you want in the physical world.

The process of creating your own reality starts with two types of questions—namely (1) the ability to directly ask for something you want; and (2) being able to propose (i.e., create) a new opportunity that benefits someone other than just yourself.

The difference between the two is that an ask generally manifests as a question that starts with, "Can I/you...?" while a proposal often begins with, "How about we...?"

While most people are unafraid to ask for things they perceive as safe bets, most will shy away from opportunities that require them to go beyond their comfort zone. For many people, the pain of potential social rejection outweighs any upside they may gain from securing a new personal relationship, business partnership, or venture.

However, this keeps people stuck at their current level of personal and professional development because they're unwilling or unable to stretch themselves beyond their existing comfort zone. In other words, they are merely asking to participate in sure shot opportunities that either match or undershoot their current skill set and capabilities rather than creating novel personal and business opportunities that demand feeling uncomfortable (but which will cause them to greatly grow in mindset and capability).

Examples of situations where people could significantly elevate their lives to a new level if they just harnessed their courage and asked the necessary questions, include approaching investors for your start-up, asking a lucrative prospective client account for their business, or creating new professional and personal relationships (or redefining existing ones) that are more win-win than everyone involved could have imagined at the start.

One problem is that too many people underestimate themselves. Specifically, they not only undervalue their own skills, experience, and perspectives, but they also—even in cases where they accurately see their own value—think that others will not recognize their merit. In my consulting practice working with very accomplished founders and senior executives, I've seen this manifest itself as missed chances, stunted professional growth, and above all, regret.

Asking the question rarely causes harm—it is the non-asking of a question out of fear of rejection that causes more damage than anything else.

Instead, many people will try to overly rely on passive signaling and credentialism. This includes getting expensive (and sometimes unnecessary) MBAs or leaning too heavily on showcasing past job experience at well-known brands to try to create new opportunities rather than taking the direct (and more effective) route of just "asking for the sale" even if they don't yet feel 100% qualified. It is of course better to have a track record and formal credentials, but oftentimes we don't 'feel' ready, even if we are ready, which leads us to not asking.

I can speak from personal experience as I have a graduate degree in law. Yet aside from the one time I was hired at my previous law firm, my credential has never ever factored into helping me secure any subsequent employment or consulting opportunity. Instead, what has helped every time is me opening my mouth and asking the other person for the chance to work together.

An example of how my own trajectory was transformed by asking and proposing a win-win arrangement was shortly after I had finished my undergraduate studies (with a degree in economics and English literature) and looking to upgrade my journalism experience to the national level in Canada.

While I had been working for local and regional publications all throughout school, I did not have a journalism degree that was often a formal prerequisite for getting hired at the largest brand name publications.

Rather than try the front door by applying directly with my CV to the top magazines in the country, I instead decided to sidestep the competition by doing what most people (including journalism grads) were afraid of: cold calling.

I intended to ask for, and propose, to create an opportunity on my own terms. I aimed for the top by targeting publications owned by what was then Canada's largest magazine publisher and proposed over a series of cold calls to the editor in chiefs (and their second in commands) of two major business magazines that they simultaneously hire me as an unpaid intern for both of their publications even though neither of them had taken interns before.

It wasn't my writing portfolio (which was decent, though not great compared to journalism grads who had work experience at top publications in Canada, the US, and Asia) that got me in. Instead, what impressed both editor in chiefs was my willingness to contact them directly out of the blue and then to propose a novel arrangement that made it worth their while to say yes to me.

If you're wondering why I proposed to work on an unpaid basis, it was because I wanted to make it impossible for either publication to refuse my offer. In exchange, I got two well recognized brand names on my CV.

Later, I asked again and proposed a new arrangement—that I convert my status as an unpaid intern to that of a paid writer.

The simple act of asking for a chance and then proposing a novel arrangement that benefited people other than myself (in this case, both magazines got a hungry, motivated, young journalist) had a transformative effect on my career when a few years later, I was hired by a global top-10 law firm (which later led to my role as a manager with significant responsibilities for major Asian markets at a global software company).

In bringing me on, the law firm hiring partners commented that they liked my gumption in cold calling two of the largest business magazines in Canada and creatively proposing that they both hire me simultaneously as well as create brand new positions specifically for me. Lawyers, after all, needed the core skill of sales in order to generate business for their firm, and this was a perfect demonstration of creating a profitable opportunity from scratch.

The point I want to make with my career example is that it pays to ask and propose. This is doubly true (and effective) because so few other people do it. Doing the things that other people fear, automatically makes you differentiated and memorable (the very things you need to stand out in this very competitive world).

Understand that most people are more than willing—and in fact—glad to help you. This is provided you make it easy for them to say yes, which most people sadly fail to do.

How do you make it easy for someone to say yes to you? If, for example, you're asking your boss for a major promotion, come prepared to your meeting with a file containing a complete list of quantifiable outcomes you've produced for the company, testimonials from clients and colleagues, and cost of living calculations along with a crystal clear outline of how you intend to create tangible results for your team in the new role. (I can personally attest to the efficacy of this method.)

Put simply, make it easy for the other person and do the heavy lifting ahead of time for them.

Overall, whether or not you can live a successful life on your personal terms (rather than merely passively accepting what's divvied out to you) is dependent on whether you can do the difficult things that make you stand out.

If this is you, then there's no getting around asking and volunteering yourself for opportunities. As the Pareto 80/20 Rule reminds us, the top opportunities go to only a small sliver of the world's population.

Therefore, there is no trick or shortcut to living a life you dictate; taking action by asking *is* the shortcut. You need to do the simple, but emotionally frightening, action of "asking for the sale," even in situations where you feel you're not ready. This is particularly important for nonrecurring opportunities which come just once and then disappear if you don't capitalize on it right away. Go ahead and experience the sweaty palms and nervousness—and do it anyway.

If you're so nervous to the point where this feels impossible, you can practice via lower stakes interactions in your daily life to build up your courage. For example, you can stretch yourself by asking your colleagues and friends for small, but somewhat uncomfortable, favors.

The goal of creating your reality is to make possible the previously impossible by asking for what scares you. For many people, asking is simple in theory, but difficult in practice. This is exactly why you want to do it—it's a competitive advantage in a world where so few others can muster the courage to withstand potentially ego-crushing rejections in order to ultimately generate unique, transformative opportunities.

INCREASE YOUR OPTIONS TO NEVER AGAIN BE HELD HOSTAGE BY MAKE-OR-BREAK SITUATIONS

Now we'll talk about perhaps the most powerful way to ensure that you continue to keep yourself out of the box: by generating optionality in your life so that you can achieve a state of outcome detachment.

What do I mean by outcome detachment? It means having multiple options at your disposal so that you never fall victim to a "make-or-break" situation.

For example, let's say your goal as a business owner is to achieve $25 million in new revenue. Rather than relying on any one single method (e.g., paid search traffic), you instead diversify across multiple avenues such as content marketing, an outbound sales force, social media, and joint ventures.

You don't sweat things because you have multiple ways of achieving your goal, so psychologically you're more confident and clear thinking because your mind isn't deleteriously clouded by the fear and anxiety of having narrow options.

If you are an employee, increasing your optionality could mean having a side business and other revenue streams–which means you're able to take greater risks in your day job such as speaking up or taking bold actions that make you stand out as a high potential hire. (I know this from personal experience.)

It's similar to how having multiple job offers means you are more likely to get at least one of them because you are more relaxed, easygoing, and not desperate (which hiring managers can pick up on).

You can also apply this principle to your personal life. For example, instead of having only one identity as a successful businessperson, you also actively cultivate additional identities as a parent to your children, child to your parents, neighbor, non-fiction writer, and marathon runner.

I'm sure you've heard stories of very successful people (including billionaires) who committed suicide because they lost their fortune, business, or job–and with it, their entire identity as a human being. The way to avoid this is to create optionality by diversifying in both your business and personal life.

By combining the principles of increased optionality with creating your reality in your professional and personal life, you not only spread your risk, but also, more importantly, you are no longer beholden to any one identity, person, partner, or outcome. You become, quite naturally, freer because no single thing has a stranglehold on you. Specifically, you become more free to take risks, try new things, and to fail while being fully aware that you will not be wiped out by any one thing.

The above examples are variations of what expert Jay Abraham in his foundational marketing treatise *Getting Everything You Can Out of All You've Got* calls the "Parthenon Principle." The Parthenon is an ancient Greek temple in Athens that is supported by multiple stone pillars. This means the structure will not collapse even if several of these supports were removed at the same time.

Having optionality is the same idea—you build structural integrity, strength, and diversification into your life to defend against unexpected (as well as expected) shocks that otherwise would have taken you down. Once you have this structural resilience, you automatically gain optionality, and hence, freedom to live your life on your terms instead of being forced to abide by someone else's agenda because you have no palatable alternative.

Yet another additional benefit of deliberately introducing optionality into your life is that it forces you to think more expansively. Rather than relying exclusively on one method that may be rendered obsolete or ineffective if circumstances suddenly change, you'll be compelled to creatively think of multiple ways to accomplish the same outcome.

We've discussed a few examples above, but what are some real-world practical ways to build outcome detachment for the long-term?

The first thing to note is that you must truly have real options. In other words, your brain isn't so stupid that you can trick it over the long-term into believing it has real optionality. It's very hard to fake having options.

One real-world way to increase optionality and achieve ongoing outcome detachment in your life is to expand your contacts beyond your normal network by cultivating "weak ties." These are relationships in industries, functions, languages, and geographies outside your usual associations.

If you think back to your own life, you'll notice that many of your biggest opportunities came not necessarily from those closest to you (people such as your family and friends with whom you already share many similar or overlapping skills, contacts, and experiences). Rather, they came from those further outside your immediate circle.

From the viewpoint of these individuals outside your usual professional and social associations (such as the college roommate of your overseas ex-colleague), assets you possess that may be commonplace in your normal circles may instead be highly valuable and rare. Think of it as a form of arbitrage: By simply changing the context, you transform what is an everyday commodity into something scarce and potentially lucrative.

This is why your greatest and most transformational opportunities may come from what either seem to be serendipitous circumstances or from people you may not necessarily be that similar to or close with.

To amplify the effect of weak ties, consider taking a global approach to scouting and identifying your upcoming big opportunities. We live in an increasingly interconnected age, and it would be foolish to artificially restrict our potential by constraining ourselves by geography, time zones, and languages along overly narrow lines.

In my own life, this means I have deliberately designed my consulting practice as one that is well diversified by serving a bilingual (English and Chinese) global client base in both the hardware and software spaces. Unlike many consultants who focus on building their business to only serve familiar time zones, I don't rely on any one industry, geography, or type of client.

This optionality means I'm not hostage to any particular client. I always have the option of maintaining my freedom because I've developed the ability to serve different client profiles around the world at any one time and in more than one language.

Finally, consider how you can redefine and reinvent existing opportunities by transplanting into the markets you serve what has already been proven to work successfully in other industries or parts of the world, but not yet being used by your competition.

You can also combine what is successful in other geographies or industries with what is already successful in your niche to create powerful new hybrid approaches that have never been seen before by your clients and customers. In this way, you gain access to a stream of novel, high-potential ideas that are waiting to be adapted and introduced as fresh and highly differentiated ways to serve the market.

CONSISTENTLY BEAT YOUR COMPETITION BY LEANING INTO YOUR KILLER INSTINCT

Similar to the concept of creating your reality, approaching opportunities in life with a killer instinct means actively and knowingly confronting things you fear and doing it anyway (rather than running or hiding from them) while also intelligently protecting your downside.

Having a killer instinct is more than what most people think of as ambition. Instead, you approach things with the mindset of seeing them through to the end at a speed that is at least quick enough to keep up with your competitors (but preferably faster). At the same time, you keep your opportunity antenna up for more promising alternatives you can transition over to if needed.

Put another way, it means assertively capitalizing on opportunities—but doing so flexibly. It means you focus and marshal your energy and attention to play full-out to achieve your desired outcome at speed, but that you simultaneously keep an eye out for alternative ways to accomplish your goal.

Actively look for new challenges that are beyond your current skill set and which will require you to elevate your thinking, courage, and mindset. This discomfort is a positive sign—it means you are growing and challenging yourself in a way that is novel for your brain, causing it to send chemical signals of anxiety, fear, and unease. Realize that it is just your brain doing what it has been programmed over millions of years of evolution to do: to keep you safe, comfortable, and stuck exactly where you are now.

Consistently training and acting on your killer instinct translates into you having real world impact on a broader and larger scale than before. For example, this could mean working on more geographically diverse projects with larger deal sizes than before. It also raises your ability to deliver within increasingly tighter timelines for more demanding clients and successfully manage larger stakes where the consequences of both failure and success are more consequential in the aggregate.

Doing this over and over means you drive a virtuous cycle where your skill and mental barriers are continually stretched, developing your capacity to take on the next more difficult challenge.

If we use video game phraseology, it means actively and knowingly choosing to play life "on hard mode." As has been said before, life is easy when you don't run from the hard things, but hard when you live it too easily.

To give you a recent example from my own life of facing the pain and doing it anyway, I had only two weeks to write this chapter while juggling my regular international client work and also taking two business classes. However, writing this chapter means I will reap the dividends for many years to come because I will have a book co-written alongside several esteemed co-authors that I can use to differentiate myself to my current and prospective clients and business partners from around the world.

This experience has also helped me develop the skill of writing books quickly within a very short time span, which is extremely valuable as I embark on my journey as a solo author.

However, you need to keep your standards high if you want to continue to play long-term at the highest level. This necessitates constant grooming and sharpening of your mindsets, cognitive thinking processes, skills, and capabilities because your competition is also constantly improving themselves.

Then there is also the danger of you retreating from hard mode once you've left the structure of a premade, demanding environment. For example, this often happens when people leave the structures of a top consulting firm, tech company, or bank.

How, then, do you keep your killer instinct? The answer is that you need to deliberately build structures that require you to play on hard mode.

For instance, I kept the same around-the-clock hours from my law firm days throughout my transition into tech. In my current consulting practice, I keep busy by setting an 'extracurricular' schedule of non-fiction reading related to my work, self-development courses, professional associations (such as mastermind groups), and teaching. I continue to work on weekends, evenings, and most holidays. This is what works for me personally and how I express my personal version of playing to win in the areas that are most important to me in my current stage of life (more on this in a later section).

All of these decisions naturally act as a forcing function to keep my instincts and mind sharp, yet they must all be deliberately planned and incorporated into my life. I do not leave these to chance.

An important part of playing to win is minimizing your risk and knowing how to fail fast. It's knowing when to cut your losses so that you're not throwing good effort after bad since your ultimate goal is to invest only in profitable opportunities. A killer instinct is not persisting stupidly and with reckless abandon—it's about applying maximum effort in effective, efficient, and intelligent ways.

If you ever experience a down period where you lose your confidence and will to win, one suggestion is to think back to past successes in your personal and professional life, no matter how long ago. My personal experience is that our brains do a poor job of distinguishing between a success from a year ago versus one from (for example) 10 years ago. To our brains, a win is a win, regardless of when it occurred. Therefore, meditate on and re-experience in your mind and body how you felt when you were successful during those past situations.

Another thing that dampens our killer instinct is doubt. This often happens when we assume we're the only person who doesn't know. In other words, we assume everyone else except us knows what to do or we wrongly think we have nothing (or little) to offer others. Therefore, we don't even want to raise our hand because we don't want to look stupid or incompetent.

This consequently causes us to not actively put ourselves forward for promising opportunities as often as we should. But you shouldn't think like this because you probably do have at least one thing (and possibly more than one) that is valuable to others. This is even if the other person ostensibly appears a lot more accomplished and successful than you.

An example is one of my clients, an experienced professional with several decades of experience. He came to me for help on troubleshooting his sales process for the start-up he had founded. Even though he had an abundance of experience advising, operating, and captaining several already established companies as a CEO and board member, he had very little hands-on experience building a company from scratch and personally pitching his product. The fact that he had at least 20 years of high quality working experience over me, yet came to me for advice, really drove home for me that we almost always have something to offer others from our areas of expertise.

Finally, make the conscious decision to be preeminent. This means deciding to become the most capable version of yourself and to always maintain and cultivate the power of agency around creating the necessary transformation in your life as changing times and circumstances demand.

FINE-TUNE YOUR LIFE STAGES FOR TRUE CONTROL OVER YOUR FUTURE

In business, there is the concept of the owner versus operator mindset. This is, respectively, the difference between working *on* your business (the long-term, big picture strategic plan) versus working *in* it (the day-to-day tactical tasks). You should adopt a similar mindset for your life to make sure you're not just focusing on your day-to-day to-dos but also stepping back to plan out where you want to go from a macro perspective, along with how you'll do it.

To do so, break your life into its key constituent segments. You can define it however you want, but you at least want to consider the key components: professional, personal (family and friends), and health (physical and emotional).

Then you decide how much time, energy, and resources you want to devote to each of these life segments. It's completely alright if you devote the bulk of your energy to one specific life segment (e.g., your professional life) if that's what you want. The goal is that you are doing this consciously—that is you are choosing the level of commitment based on what you decide is best for you.

The reason you want to break your life down into its constituent segments is so that you can not only see from a high level how you are currently spending your time and energy, but also to know where you can reallocate your resources if you feel your life isn't where it should (or can) be. In other words, you're giving yourself the tools to plan your different life segments in a highly structured and granular way.

Next, break your life into chronological stages where each one can be as long or short as you want. You then allocate percentages to relevant life segments in each life stage you've identified.

A key part of this is to give yourself full permission to focus on as few or many of the life segments as you want. For example, one person may want to split their time 30-60-10 between professional development, family, and their physical health, respectively. Meanwhile, another person may decide to go all-in on their career with an 80-20 split between their career and health (physical and emotional).

Putting things together and looking at this more broadly, this could mean you set a foundational stage running from age 22 to 35 where you focus almost entirely on your career. During this phase, you work hard to acquire the skills and contacts needed to start your own business from age 36 onward. At the same time, in the latter half of this foundational phase, you also start to seriously explore the possibility of starting a family.

Then, in the subsequent stage from age 36 to 50 (let's call this the consolidation stage), you focus on balancing your family responsibilities with working hard at your business so that by 51 you can consider a form of semi-retirement (perhaps called the self-exploration stage).

Choose what you want based on your desired trajectory. It doesn't matter: Choose your life stages and their respective durations based on what works for you.

In other words, you assign prioritization and sequencing to your life's stages based on where you are in your life and where you want to be in the future. Doing so allows you to plan backward from a specific objective so that you can better judge how to apportion your time, energy, and concentration.

And again, as I have emphasized throughout this chapter, we do this so that you can consciously shape how you live your life, rather than leaving it to how your family, friends, business partners, and society want you to live.

Does this mean that things will turn out exactly as you plan them? Certainly not, since it's impossible to know exactly how the future will turn out. As the saying goes, no plan survives contact with the enemy.

But what this exercise does is that it gives you a structure for planning specific chronological phases of your life in the same way that the years starting from middle school to university graduation are typically much more structured with key milestones. For most people, this would be general and specific timelines around key "coming of age" activities such as studying for standardized exams, applying for postsecondary institutions, participating in extracurriculars to bolster their entrance applications, and then finally, attending job fairs toward the end of their college experience.

However, most people will generally lose this type of structure upon leaving school and entering the working world, which leads many of them to drift unconsciously in their personal and professional lives.

This is why it's important to have at least some sort of basic plan in place so that you can set an overall direction to guide your day-to-day actions. This ultimately allows you to move progressively closer toward living your desired life.

In sum, breaking your life down into its key segments and chronological phases means planning things out as you would in business project management by assigning project focuses, activities, timelines, and resource allocations. As I said before, it's impossible to predict where you will be in the next five to ten years, but at least you have a general direction, which is much better than zero planning.

In sum, planning your life in sequenced, timeboxed stages (as well as decomposing each individual stage into prioritized key life segments) means you are able to finetune your life with a degree of detail and granular thoughtfulness that eludes most people—even those very successful by traditional measures.

The edge you'll have over others (and yourself) is that you'll be living your life very consciously instead of completely on the fly and at the mercy of randomness.

You will, in other words, live your life with the power of agency and conscious deliberation, which is atypical in our society.

HOW TO LIVE CONGRUENTLY WITH YOURSELF

The final step is to define the principles of how you will live and the purpose for why you do what you do.

Your principles and purpose are personal to you so when you come up with them, make sure they reflect who you are and what you believe, not what you think you should believe.

Similar to what we discussed in the section on breaking out of the box, the only restriction is that they are not illegal or harmful to others.

As examples, here are some of my personal principles:

- I will always first create value for others in my professional and personal relationships and will not expect anything in return.
- I will never rely on any one client and will instead have multiple streams of revenue.
- I will walk away from any relationship that is not a good fit for me regardless of how much time, energy, and money I have already invested.
- I cultivate business and personal contacts that span the globe

rather than be restricted to any one geography.

Your goal in determining your personal principles is to elucidate the specific, granular values that truly reflect what you believe so that when you go out into the physical world to bring your reality into existence, you are always congruent with who you are.

As for your purpose, another CEO client of mine (this time in the real estate software business) once asked me what question is rarely asked by entrepreneurs, senior executives, and professionals, but which should be raised more often.

I told him that we don't spend the time or effort to find out what truly motivates us on a deep, primal, emotional level. In other words, we don't ask ourselves, "What would I do for free?" often enough. As clichéd as this question is, it's important to find what truly fuels our motivational fire.

For me, it's learning and mastering (or at least gaining baseline understanding of) challenging and difficult skills that are in-demand by the market. This includes high leverage 'horizontal' skills that can be applied across different industries and life segments including relationship management, writing, public speaking, marketing, sales, and non-linear thinking. There's an inherent joy and flow state I experience when I do what drives me at a deep emotional level.

So, ask yourself what is it that truly drives you on a deep, pre-verbal level that you can't necessarily logically explain with your intellectual mind. A good test of this is if you answer, "I just like it," without being able to explain why you like it. That's a strong sign that you've hit upon something that motivates you at a deep, primal, and emotional level where you don't need to necessarily push yourself all that much using motivational slogans ("Just do it!") or with abundant willpower (which is not sustainable anyway).

For true sustained and long-term drive, you need to tap into what motivates you emotionally (and this is coming from someone who thinks heavily from the left-brain analytical side).

Your purpose is something you devote yourself to working on over the long-term for the rest of your life (or a phase of your life as explained in the life stages section).

One thing to keep in mind is that your purpose and set of principles are not meant to lock you into rigid ways of thinking or acting. Instead, they provide a set of general guardrails to ensure you don't participate in opportunities or relationships that either don't suit you, take you off your trajectory, or which actively hurt you or others.

Be sure, therefore, to keep yourself open to new and unexpected opportunities that were not originally on your radar as long as they are compatible with your principles and purpose. As you may have already personally experienced, some of the most transformational events in our lives stem from the most unexpected–and sometimes serendipitous–occurrences.

SUMMARY

Leadership over yourself and for those in your life, starts in your mind. More specifically, it has to do with understanding that the ways you currently think and act are probably already shaped by ideas and customs implanted in us for better or worse by society, family, friends, culture, and schooling (among other things). These invisible walls have been built up in us over years (and perhaps decades), often via osmosis, without us thinking about the immediate or downstream implications on our life and on the lives of those we interact with. Some benefit us, while others disadvantage us.

Living a business and personal life decided on your personal terms requires that you first recognize these influences and then consciously decide to break out of the box.

Once you've escaped, you need to set about actually creating the life you want in the physical world. To do this, directly ask for the opportunities you want and propose beneficial win-win arrangements that make it impossible for the other person to say no to you.

If you feel anxious, then feel the fear and do it anyway because it's a massive advantage in a world where passivity and taking the safe, easy route is your competition's default behavior. Developing your killer instinct requires that you do the things that scare you so that you can continually sharpen your capabilities to create increasingly better outcomes for yourself and for those around you.

A key way to increase your freedom is to actually have real alternative options for achieving your objectives. In other words, you can't fool your brain over the long-term into outcome detachment. More options results in greater outcome detachment, which consequently means you'll enjoy greater power over yourself and external situations.

Make sure you have a systematic plan for how you will allocate your time and energy by splitting your life into chronological stages corresponding to where you are right now while also taking into account your future ambitions and goals.

Finally, elucidate your key principles for how you will live as well as your purpose for why you live. What your principles and purpose are as a leader both to yourself and to those in your life are entirely up to you as long as they don't break any of your society's laws or harm others.

More than anything, the set of ideas and ways of thinking, being, and living introduced in this chapter are all about opening your mind to enable you to take bold action to achieve what's possible at the outermost edge of life. In other words, the most exciting part of life.

AUTHOR BIO

Richmond Wong works directly with founders and senior leadership of international start-ups on their highest ROI leadership, product, and growth initiatives.

Having launched multiple complex B2B platforms for Reuters and LexisNexis in 10+ developed and emerging markets including Hong Kong, Singapore, Korea, Taiwan, Malaysia and throughout Southeast Asia, Richmond brings both a high-level and "from the trenches" perspective on international leadership to all his client engagements.

His clients include a growing list of software and hardware companies from the US, Australia, Hong Kong, and Canada.

Richmond is also a Teaching Assistant for MBA-level courses taught by handpicked Wharton, Cornell, New York University, and UC Berkeley professors at Section4, a NYC-based edtech start-up founded by CNN's Scott Galloway.

Richmond has lectured on product principles at Royal Dutch Shell's LiveWIRE accelerator and at San Francisco-headquartered Product School.

Before moving into tech, Richmond trained as a corporate lawyer with one of the world's 10 largest law firms, Hogan Lovells, serving Fortune 500 clients on their most mission critical mandates.

Richmond started his career as a journalist with Rogers Publishing, then Canada's largest magazine group.

Connect With Richmond: For free articles, updates, and case studies on how to improve your personal and professional leadership skills, visit www.richmondwong.com.

CHAPTER 5

Leadership Empowered by Communication

BY ALICE QINHUA ZHOU

I **LANDED IN NEW YORK** at the JFK airport on July 9, 2009. The US Custom Officer greeted me with, "How are you?" I gave him a two-minute run down of how tiring the trip was. When he asked me why I came to the US, I said I would like to win a Nobel Prize one day. My thesis was on hardcore physics related to the modeling of atom-atom interactions in proteins. I rarely spoke to anyone other than my Ph.D. advisors. That 2009 Alice had thought the physical world was logical, but humans were less logical and were hard to deal with. Ten years later, I am a management consultant in back-to-back meetings all day long, solving business problems, and helping executives in financial institutions drive sustainable and profitable growth for their companies. Every minute of my day revolves around engaging people—clients and team members in different countries with different educational and cultural backgrounds, years of experience, agendas, personalities, and capabilities. As you can imagine, the transition was not easy.

The stories you will read are the key communication lessons I wish I had known 10 years ago. I will lay out those lessons by sharing my mistakes, actionable tips, and the science behind them. Of course, I have changed the client names to protect their identities, but this will not impact your reading experience.

I hope these lessons will help you be more successful in achieving the results you desire–whether that is to get promoted faster, build executive relationships, sell more services, build your personal brand, or effectively manage up, down, or across. At the minimum, I am confident that these lessons will make your journey to become an effective leader much easier by showing you how to avoid the mistakes that I made (or save on the numerous $400 per hour of psychologist consultations you may need throughout your transition).

LESSON 1: COMMUNICATION IS COMPLEX, CREATING ROOM FOR MISINTERPRETATIONS

You can imagine how hard it was for me, a non-native English speaker, to understand what others truly meant in the first few years in the US. For example, I would always pause for a few seconds in the first couple of months when someone asked, "How are you?" Similarly to how I replied to that US Customs Officer, I thought they truly wanted to know how I was feeling, and it was hard to summarize it all in one sentence. One day, I saw two ladies meeting in the hallway: One woman smiled and said, "How are you?" and the other replied, "How are you?" They passed each other, and the conversation ended! It made me realize that I may have wasted that poor US Custom Officer's time, as well as the time of countless people by telling them how I was actually doing.

Thanks to my struggles in the early days, I learned the hard way that communication is complex as everyone could have their own interpretations due to their upbringing, educational background, and work experience. Let's consider a conversation between two persons like a game of passing words at each other, like passing balls. When we use a word, we have all the history, story, and interpretations attached to the word. Think of the interpretation as a high-definition movie containing everything we've experienced and learned over time (consciously or subconsciously). When we say the word or throw the 'ball' at the other person, our 'movie' gets detached from the ball and lost in the transition. When the other person hears the words or catches the 'ball,' they must then interpret the word using their experience and create their version of the 'movie.' That version may be very different from what you are trying to communicate. You may have seen the image "My Wife and My Mother-in-Law," a famous optical illusion that depicts both an old woman looking off to the left and a young woman facing away, looking over her right shoulder. The picture is the same, but the interpretation is different.

This plays out in the real world all the time. During a client interview, I once asked one of my clients, Bobby, "Why did the cycle time increase in the past six months?" He felt offended and said that I was accusing him of not being capable of solving the problem. What just happened? The ball was the word 'why.' My movie attached to the word 'why' was "what is the reason," as my English teacher had taught me in elementary school. However, when I threw the ball at Bobby, he created a different movie. Perhaps the 'why' reminded him of when his mother yelled at him, "Why did you do that!?" after he spilled the milk all over the floor at age six. He attached that movie to the 'why' word and interpreted the 'why' as an accusation.

To minimize similar misinterpretations, I found it critical to consider the countless possible interpretations behind the words and choose words, sentence structure, and tones carefully. I always ask myself

- Would a six-year-old kid or an 80-year-old grandma understand what I am saying?
- How will the most sensitive people in the world react to my sentence?
- What are all the other possible (negative) ways for them to interpret what I say?

We all know that the risk of misinterpretations in communication can be high, especially in a business setting. But you may wonder, "I don't have the same background as others," or, "I am not inside others' brains; how can I possibly predict how others will interpret or internalize my words?" Here are my two cents:

- Observe: When you are in a conversation, ask yourself, "What is the difference in word choices between their and my way of expressing the same meaning?" When you read their documents, notice the frequently used words or the words they avoid using. For example, if you are talking to an insurance executive, do they refer to the payment to the insurance policyholders as claim loss (P&C insurance), benefits (life insurance), or MedEx (health insurance)? Are their consumers referred to as customers, clients, members, policyholders, or something else?

- Rephrase and playback: Say something like, "I want to make sure what I heard is correct," or "Do you mean X by Y?" and listen to their reactions (see more tips in Lesson 4).
- Copy or mimic: Adapt their vocabulary and use their interpretation or version of the words when talking to them.
- Get feedback: Be open and solicit feedback from the start. For example, "I am new to your organization. Words can have different meanings. Let me know if there are any expressions you would suggest me to convey differently." You will be surprised at how willing others are to help you, even in the first meeting. For example, a business unit (BU) leader in a Midwest company, Joe, once told me never to use the phrase "enterprise-wide" because it meant 'centralized' in this company and had a negative connotation in their federated organization structure. (By the way, asking him to provide coaching made him feel in control and respected. We will get back to this point in Lesson 4.)
- Read novels: Develop empathy by reading fictional novels; some writers are good at portraying internal emotion and thoughts during a conversation. If you immerse yourself and feel what the character feels, you could experience many different backgrounds or ways of thinking.

LESSON 2: COMMUNICATION IS AN "INFINITE GAME"

Communication is an "infinite game," not a finite one. I borrowed this "infinite game" concept from Professor James Carse's book *Finite and Infinite Game*. What is the difference between an infinite versus finite 'game?' The goal of a finite one is to win. There are defined rules with boundaries for location, time, and participants. For example, a football match or a debate will end, and some participant(s) will be declared a winner. On the contrary, the goal of an "infinite game" is to extend the event as much as possible. The video game Tetris for example, is an infinite game. The fun part of the game is keeping the game going for as long as possible. Running a business is more or less an infinite game as well. The goal is to keep the business running, surviving, and growing through the market cycles, disruptive innovation, and competitors.

Similar to the game *Tetris*, communication could be viewed as an infinite game. The goal of communication is to keep the conversation going and sustain the relationship.

Let's take a look at a story of turning a losing situation into building a long-standing relationship when having the mindset of an "infinite game" for communication.

A financial institution issued a request for proposal (RFP) to conduct a benchmarking study for their expenses. The client had very diversified lines of businesses, making it challenging to find comparable peers. However, my firm felt very strongly that providing benchmarking would be misleading and prevent the client from achieving their objectives.

By reading between the lines of the RFP document, we realized that the client was facing capital pressure to fund digital investment. Their goal was to use benchmarks to set cost reduction targets that would help create investment capacity to launch the program.

Instead of offering the benchmarking study requested in the RFP response, we proposed to focus on solving their fundamental needs of funding digital investments and increasing operating margin—preventing expense growth from outpacing revenue growth. We laid out our approach to create and execute a successful enterprise transformation aimed at bending the cost curve and sustaining profitable growth. Since we genuinely did not believe benchmarks would benefit them, we also shared the potential risks associated with using benchmarks and included the points that they must pay attention to when interpreting benchmarks, should they still plan to go down that route.

Although we did not win the benchmark study, the CFO, Steve, was intrigued by our response and asked to meet over breakfast for 30 minutes. We did not have a relationship with Steve prior to the breakfast, nor had we had a strong relationship with his company. The client had been using another strategy firm as their exclusive consulting partner for strategic programs. While they had spent millions of dollars with the competing firms, Steve's company only hired us for a total of around $200,000 in consulting services over the prior five years.

During the breakfast, we listened to his needs and addressed his concerns across various aspects of the enterprise transformation. The breakfast originally scheduled for just 30 minutes became a 90-minute conversation. What I remember most vividly about that conversation was the moment we discovered that Steve's company had recently sold one of their businesses to a client we had served before. Steve immediately texted the CFO of our client, Peter, and asked for his advice and experience. While we were still at breakfast, Steve received a response from Peter saying, "Hire the person in front of you if you want to get results. Give me a ring."

In the end, we were named as the sole partner for all of their multi-year enterprise strategic transformation programs due to our understanding of the client's underlying needs and our performance track record. Over time, we further developed a strong, trusted partnership across their leadership team and helped them achieve their strategic objectives. Even today, the client continues to engage us on all their strategic programs.

Looking back, if we viewed the communication with Steve as a "finite game," we easily could have declined to bid on the project or tried to win by just providing exactly what they asked for in the RFP, even though we knew it wasn't the right answer for Steve or his company. Instead, we built a long-standing relationship and kept the conversation going beyond the RFP by answering their questions honestly; by responding to the RFP with our viewpoints, we planted the seed in the CFO's head that we understood their needs and had the experience to be able to support the entire strategic transformation program. Not only that, but Steve has also been one of our most avid supporters in providing references to CFOs of our prospective clients, which has opened up even more opportunities for us—all stemming from the relationship and credibility we were able to establish and maintain with Steve.

Now that you have heard my story, how can you apply this "infinite game" concept to build long-standing relationships in your daily life?

- Stay in touch, especially with your clients and mentors. Those who liked you and helped you in the past are more likely to help you again. Think about this: Would Peter still remember us and refer us to Steve if we didn't stay in touch with him? Probably not. It could be viewed as transactional if you only reach out when you want or need something from the other person. Staying in touch doesn't necessarily require long, back-and-forth messages; a simple, short text can be enough. For example, "I saw an article in *Harvard Business Review* today, and I think the article raises a few interesting points that may be relevant for you. Here is the link."

- Treat every interaction as an opportunity to learn more about the other person and deepen the relationship; at the minimum, be aware of the possibility of collaborating again, and do everything you can to avoid "burning a bridge" or "creating an enemy."
- Don't be afraid of failure; as long as you don't "burn the bridge," you can always adjust your approach. Keep in mind that your journey will continue for as long as you are alive; you can always improve, creating a better you today than yesterday, which will later create opportunities for you tomorrow.

LESSON 3: BE HELPFUL TO OTHERS BY DISCOVERING THEIR PROFESSIONAL NEEDS

In the previous lesson, one of the major reasons why we won Steve's trust is because we demonstrated our understanding of his needs—another key lesson I wish I had known earlier in my career.

When I first started consulting, I thought the clients hired us to solve problems. But that is often not the reason, or at least, not the only reason. Yes, there are cases where the sponsor doesn't know the answer. For example, Steve may not have been familiar with all the operational areas as a CFO. He needed help to overcome organizational barriers to find out the transformation ideas within operations, apply our lessons learned elsewhere, or trust us to be smart enough to solve the problem from the first principles. However, when we started the project, it soon became evident that everyone we talked to had their answers. What they were missing was not the answers, but often the endorsement or resources from a third party to help them tell the story better and thereby sell their solutions within the organization.

I still remember my first cost reduction project with a large national bank in 2015. Sarah, the head of the call center, was not cooperative. She cited "negative impact for customer experience" and "downgrades to quality" as possible negative impacts of reducing costs and therefore she was not cooperating in the project. We struggled to engage her until the day we saw her Monthly Business Report (MBR) to the CEO. In the MBR, her call center was suffering from high attrition; her hiring couldn't keep up, and thus, her service level goal (80% of calls answered in 20 seconds) was not met.

With her key performance indicators (KPIs) (i.e., service goal and attrition rate) and pain points in mind, we approached the conversation differently: We positioned the program as a vehicle to help her solve service level issues. Specifically, to meet the service level goal, she could attack from two angles, increase supply (i.e., staff more associates) or reduce demand (i.e., reduce the number of calls that need to be handled by associates).

To address the supply issue, she needed funding to accelerate the agent desktop integration so that associates did not have to waste time switching amongst the 10+ systems to find the answers for the customer on the phone. This integrated desktop would also shorten the training time needed for new hires from six to two weeks. On the other side, 80% of calls coming in were simple calls such as making monthly payments and changing addresses. She needed IT support to improve self-service capabilities (e.g., improve website design, chatbot, automated payment in IVR). She also needed the upstream, the sales and account teams, to improve the onboarding processes to minimize calls for new customers. Once we discovered those needs, we helped her develop the business case for the accelerated implementation of the agent desktop integration and self-service capabilities. We also worked with the sales and account team in updating onboarding processes to reduce call demand and helped IT articulate the benefits they would realize in IT operations from consolidating and migrating systems.

As you can tell from the story with Sarah, the key is to understand the needs of others and position yourself to be helpful to them. But how? How to discover their needs? Get to know them! "History never repeats itself, but it rhymes." This quote applies to individuals metaphorically as well. You could derive many hypotheses on their needs as you know them better through in-person conversations, Google, or company intranet search.

Take Sarah, for example.* You can search on LinkedIn to figure out:

- Where did she go to college and what is her past work experience? Undergrad major in political science, engineering, or finance? What's your guess on her cognitive preference or bias in decision-making? (See more details on cognitive preference in Lesson 5)

* To protect Sarah's identity, I couldn't lay out the detailed process to profile Sarah's needs.

- What is her history in the current organization? Did she just join from another company or is she a tenured employee? Did she climb up the corporation ladder from an agent or make a lateral move from another function? What is she insecure about in the position?
- What are her career aspirations? Challenges? Be a COO one day or ready to retire?
- What is her relationship/network? Do you know anyone who connects with her?

You also need to try to know them on a personal level. For example:

- What are her hobbies (e.g., music instruments, sports, vacation spots)?
- How about her family (i.e., spouse, kids), religion, political preference?**
- Does she hold any board position for non-profits?

Once you know them holistically, you can derive their objectives—both professional and personal. KPIs or OKRs (Objective and Key Results) can be found in the SEC filings or KPI dashboards. Keep in mind that there would be unspoken KPIs/OKRs, and the company's objectives may not align 100% with personal career aspirations. The last step is to identify how their objectives—whether it be KPIs, OKRs, or personal goals—overlap with yours and tell them how you can be helpful to them.

** Donation records to political parties are publicly available.

LESSON 4: ADDRESS THE EMOTIONAL NEEDS OF OTHERS

In the previous session, we talked about discovering others' professional needs and position yourself to be helpful. However, sometimes that is not enough. You also need to align the delivery of the message to serve the unspoken emotional needs. Why? The human brain is like a smartphone. The knowledge, logic, and skills parts are like the apps installed later. The emotional or psychological needs, on the contrary, are like the operating system (i.e., iOS, Android) that controls how apps run. It is easier to change the apps but hard to update the operating system. In this section, I will share a few ways to talk to the operating system, the emotional needs, which are the prerequisites before you can address their professional needs. You will find that this lesson is much longer than the other ones because it was the biggest mindset shift for me from a physicist to an advisor (or an 'unlicensed' psychologist).

I hope you still remember Maslow's hierarchy of needs in the Psychology 101 class. Here are the major layers of needs:

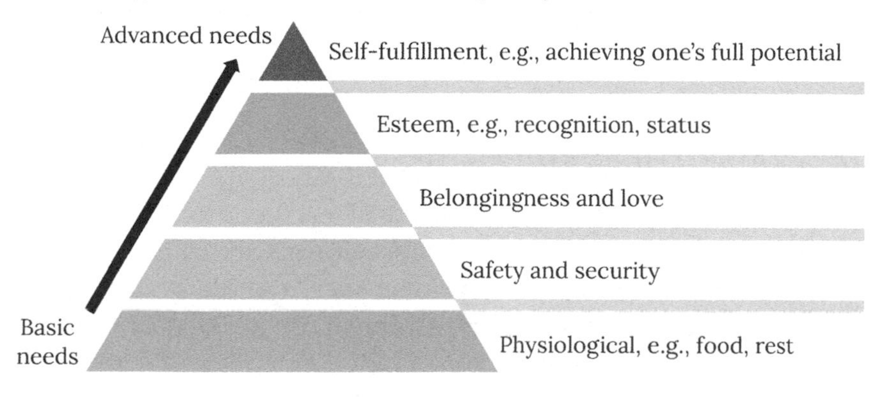

In modern societies, basic needs are often satisfied. We, as leaders, need to focus on the advanced needs such as self-fulfillment and belonging. I found the following tips helpful in successfully influencing others or building relationships. These tips help because they address fundamental emotional needs by making others feel they are seen, heard, respected, and recognized.

1. THANK THEIR ACTIONS

Appreciation makes them feel their efforts have been 'seen' and that you understand how hard they worked. The general structure is: "Thank you for the time/effort for [something they contributed], especially when [the challenges they are facing]." For example, I would say to the client, a Finance Director, who provided detailed vendor data for us, "Thank you for putting the time in pulling the vendor data. I know this was hard as you had to piece together the information from multiple general ledgers, sourcing systems during the closing period."

If you want to build a loyal team, it is important to thank them for their efforts before providing any coaching type of feedback. Put yourself into their position: When you worked until finishing a deck and sent it to your manager at 1:00 a.m., the first thing you want to hear at that time is, "Thank you! Really nice work; I appreciate the team putting all the effort into this," not heartless comments such as, "Please change the sentence on page X to..."

2. PRAISE THEIR STRENGTHS

In my experience, the biggest need of everyone is "being seen." Praising others' strengths is the most direct way of making them feel 'seen.' For the other person to "be seen," the praise needs to be specific to them. In other words, it contains details that can apply to only them. For example, compare the following four options:

- Version A: You did very well in the meeting.
- Version B: You are so good at running the meeting.
- Version C: You did very well in grounding them on the data gaps.
- Version D: You did very well in grounding them on the data gaps, so that [client] could help us accelerate the data gathering.

Version C gives specific details (vs. Version A) and praises the action, not an intrinsic capability (vs. Version B). Version D is even better because it provides the logic behind it and the impact of the action.

With that in mind, please put yourself in the other person's shoes, and be very careful and selective in what you choose to praise. Please make sure you praise what you truly believe is worth praising. In the movie *Whiplash*, the coach said, "There are no two words in the English language more harmful than 'good job.'" If you think your team can do better, tell them that. Suppose someone praises you for calculating "1+1=2" correctly; how would that make you feel? You would probably think: 1) the other person had such a low expectation of you (i.e., think you can't even get that simple calculation right), or 2) they are not sincere and don't mean what they say.

The "1+1=2" example may sound ridiculous. However, I have run into similar praises many times. For example, a partner 'praised' me, an experienced manager, for aligning the boxes in PowerPoint slides correctly. I couldn't help but feel puzzled and offended.

If you look at it from a darker perspective, praise can also be interpreted as manipulative. Parents may praise a child as a way of motivating the child to perform actions that are aligned with the parents' goals or desires. Let's be wise in using such a powerful technique in business settings.

3. LISTEN ATTENTIVELY

People are more likely to feel they are in control and respected if the other is listening to them. For example, in Lesson 1 I mentioned that asking for feedback/coaching from the other person is particularly useful. Many communication books teach techniques on how to listen, such as nodding; saying 'yeah' periodically; don't multitask; take notes on paper. However, the best listening skill you can demonstrate is to act on their advice/feedback. After all, you've heard this phrase countless times: "Actions speak louder than words." Michael, one of my mentors, once suggested I wear a red belt to an interview. He saw that I followed his advice, even though it was a minor suggestion. He told me that was the moment he found "Alice was coachable" and decided to invest more time in me.

How do you listen well? When listening, you need to look for three elements: facts, feelings, and expectations. For example, imagine your manager asks, "When will you send me that deck?" after returning from a client meeting:

- The fact is that they have not received that deck yet.
- The feeling could be, "The client is asking about the progress. I am anxious or nervous, as I haven't seen the latest version."
- Their expectation might be that they want to see the draft deck or get a progress update from you.

By analyzing those three dimensions, you could reply and address all their needs. In this example, "We set up a time to review the deck with you at 2:00 p.m. today. We're 90% done with minor tweaks left on the ABC section. Although we're still working on it, we're happy to share the current version with you if you want to see it now. Is there anything particular you're looking for?" The last sentence ensures you keep the conversation open and let them express their needs explicitly if you didn't hit the point.

4. ENCOURAGE THEM TO SHARE

The last sentence in the previous example is a way of encouraging them to give more information. In other situations, you could also say

- "I am interested in your thoughts."
- "Can you elaborate more?"
- "Do you have any questions or concerns?"
- "How can I be helpful?"
- "One solution is ...; what do you think?"

Ultimately, the goal of communication is to transmit information accurately and efficiently to achieve the same goal. Think of the 2x2 matrix below: The bigger the consensus (i.e., area A) is, the more aligned you and the other person are.

	I know	I don't know
You know	A: Consensus	B: My blind spot
You don't know	C: Your blind spot	D: Common blind spot

Everyone's favorite topic is themselves. When you give them the space and make them feel safe to share, they will share. If you let them talk more, you are going to widen area A.

How do you make them feel safe to talk? You need to know what is holding them back. What are they insecure about? What are their vulnerabilities? Take Sarah, the head of the call center we previously talked about, for example again. Was she insecure about talking to consultants because the more information she provided, the more mistakes we would have found in her organizations? Or was she worried about losing power if we came in and cut her budget? Or did she feel that she was an ineffective leader because her boss brought the consultants in to help her? Looking back today, I am sure our collaboration could have been smoother if I had closely observed how she had reacted and addressed her emotional insecurities in our very first meeting.

Another general method to make the clients feel safe is to give them a sense of belonging. Being a member of a large tribe was essential for the survival of our ancestors. Their guard will come down if you make them feel you two are similar or belong to the same group/ affiliation. Here are some of the aspects you could look out for to draw similarities (in order of difficulty to identify):

- color of their shirt, glasses, or phone cases, or any other small details when you met each other
- educational background, work experience, hobbies, etc. (recall the list toward the end of Lesson 3)
- common objectives/KPIs (particularly useful in team collaboration; recall the Sarah story in Lesson 3)
- common friends (Better used in combination with work or education background; you don't want the other person to think that you are stalking them on Facebook)
- family situation (This requires you to be open and sharing first. For example, my mom was diagnosed with pancreatic cancer in Oct 2020; it made it easier to connect with two partners and one client who lost their parents during COVID-19)
- common group subconscious (such as preconceived notions, biases)

5. PLAYBACK THEIR POINTS BETTER THAN THEY DO

There are a few benefits to playing back what you heard from the other person:

1. You avoid any chances of misinterpretations we talked about in Lesson 1.

2. If you can make their points better than they do, they feel heard or 'seen,' and that you value their opinion and thoughts. Their defensive guard will go down, and they will be more likely to open for new or additional information.

3. You make them feel they are in control of the conversation.

Let me share a story on how I messed up by not playing back. One day, my Ph.D. advisor saw the A4 paper for the printers was running out. He asked me to order 'some.' He gave me the credit card and left. I ordered 20 boxes of A4 paper; each box contains 20 stacks of paper. In other words, I bought a 5-year paper supply for our office. I am sure you could imagine how shocked my advisor was when he saw the truck arrive and unload the piles of boxes. Ever since then, he never asked me to order any office supplies. I wish I had played back to him by asking, "When you say 'some' paper, do you mean buying a few stacks or the full year worth of paper supply?"

Nowadays, my typical structure of playing back when being asked to do something is:

- To make sure I fully get what you are trying to say, can I playback? (You could use the full sentence to buy some time to think or shorten it to "to playback." The key is making sure you signal the other person that the intent of the next question is to confirm, not to challenge.)
- Do you mean [rephrase that person's ask]?
- Pause, see their reactions
- If so, I plan to do [List actions/approach]
- Is that what you have in your mind? (Open-ended, encourage them to share more, see previous session, Lesson 4.4)

You can also apply this playback concept in many other forms. For example, at the end of the meeting, I would say, "Let me summarize the key next steps or takeaways for this meeting; feel free to add in."

The second part is to encourage them to share and give them the autonomy or "in control" feeling.

Another common situation for playback is when you delegate work to your team, ask, "Could you replay what you just heard?" so that you can catch any misalignments before they spend three hours on things that you only expect to require 10 minutes to complete.

You can also use playback when you disagree with others' approaches by weaving in your alternative solution. For example, "Do you mean approach A [playback what the other said] or approach B [your idea or what they didn't say, such as their underlying needs]?" I would recommend using this only when the other person's opinion is vague or unclear, or you are in a culture where indirect expression is the common practice (e.g., Japan). Otherwise, others can quickly tell you are trying to manipulate them. The key is to clarify that the 'blame' is on yourself and make it seem like you did not fully understand what they meant and need to clarify what you heard. For example, you can preface your playback with, "To make sure I fully captured what you said or meant, could you help me understand what you mean by [XYZ]? Did you mean [approach A] or [approach B]?"

The concept of playing back also extends beyond words and sentences. Have you ever noticed a moment in a meeting when someone picks up a cup to drink water, and the rest of the meeting attendees do the same? You could also playback by mimicking their body language. Such mimicking is another way of signaling others that we are similar by matching body language. For example, next time you are in a one-on-one meeting, you could try to gradually lean on the same side as the other person. It would make the other person subconsciously sense that you two are similar or on the same page.

Lastly, these tips can be combined and mixed into one conversation. Let's take one of my meetings with Sam, the head of Underwriting from Steve's company, for example.

	Conversation	Notes
Alice:	Thank you for agreeing to connect on short notice.	Thank your contact
	I know you have a busy schedule.	Indirect Praise, confirm his power
	We would like to hear your feedback on the deck.	
Sam:	I like the business case. A lot of points there make sense. But the assumption for the auto-issue rate seems to be too high.	Notice that Sam also Praised here
Alice:	Could you say a bit more?	Encourage to share more
	Do you want to reduce it from X to Y%?	Playback
	Or do you have other concerns or thoughts in mind?	Encourage to share more
Sam:	The % is reasonable. ABC product has already reached the assumption on the deck, but the ABC product is a simplified product, and we sold most of them online.	Alice listening; nod as needed
Alice:	I understand. Are you worried that the other products may not be that successful, given brokers sell them in paper form?	Empathize, playback, ending in a question to encourage to say more
Sam:	Yes, that is only part of the issue. We don't have a good way to double-check the data on the paper applications. My team spends a lot of time opening scanned PDF to double-check names and correct mistakes made by the OCR.*	Alice listening
Alice:	I see. That is a really good point!	Praise
	We need to point out that you have a few prerequisites to achieve that auto-issue rate in the business case. The first one is... Is that what you have in mind?	Playback and suggest solutions based on your reading of his expectation
Sam:	Yes, you got me!	

* OCR is an optical character recognition application to convert handwriting to digital.

LESSON 5: TAILOR YOUR DELIVERY STYLE TO SAVE THE BRAIN'S ENERGY BUDGET

Research shows that visual cues (e.g., body language, facial expression) and vocal (e.g., tones) cues have a greater impact than verbal (e.g., what words you say) cues on whether others like you or not.*

Throughout my career, I have made numerous mistakes on this front. For example, I interviewed a BU president of a top five US asset manager. After the meeting, Jay, the partner on the project, pulled me aside and told me that I was crushing the edge of my notebook paper. Every time I did that, the BU president was distracted by me. However, I had no idea that I did that. Another piece of feedback I got was, "Speak slower" when I was nervous. As you can imagine, speaking fast plus my Chinese accent makes it hard for the other person to understand me. The key is to get feedback on the nonverbal cues that prevent you from delivering messages effectively. Videotaping yourself or practicing in front of a mirror could also help.

Our brain consumes at least 20% of our energy while resting. Thinking is an unnatural status of our brain, and it wants to find shortcuts to save energy. Therefore, you also need to take this fact into consideration when designing your communication approach. I still have a long learning journey ahead of me on this topic. Here are a few aspects to consider based on what I have learned from my own mistakes so far:

* To be precise: Total liking = 7% verbal + 38% vocal + 55% facial.

- Give options to choose: Providing multiple choices can save their brain energy compared to asking open questions.
- Ask questions: Instead of stating directly, ask the question of, "Shall we try [XYZ]?" to convey they still have the autonomy to choose. The science behind it is that when one feels you are influencing them, they will fight/resist it. You want to avoid triggering that resistance and save their brain energy. Going one step further, instead of including [XYZ] in the question, try to ask, "Have you considered [ABC]?" where if they consider [ABC], it is easier for them to reach a conclusion by themself. We are not filing for a patent; it doesn't matter who comes up with the idea. Getting others' agreement/collaboration and, ultimately, the results are what matters.
- Match their cognitive patterns: Try to understand others' cognitive patterns and communicate in the way they prefer to save brain energy. Again, the answers to the following questions can be derived from a Google search and in-person interactions (see Lesson 3). For example
    - Do they like induction reasoning (bottom-up, give the evidence first) or deduction reasoning (top-down, give the so-what first)?
    - Do they like numbers or logic more or hearing moving stories that touch their feelings?
    - Do they prefer details or the big picture?
    - Do they like direct versus indirect statements?
    - Do they prefer formal or informal tones?
    - What communication channel do they prefer? (e.g., text, phone call, email, in-person meetings in the office,

coffee shop, or shared car ride)

- Feed them sugar before engaging in conversations: The brain needs glucose to function well. You could hand them candy, chocolate, hot (not cold!) coffee with sugar (not sweetener).[**,***] You could also avoid talking to them before they had breakfast, right before lunch or right after a big meal.[****,*****]

** Research found that people judged others to be more generous and caring if they had just held a warm cup of coffee and less so if they had held an iced coffee.

*** Sweetener gives a taste of sweetness but does not contain glucose.

**** Research found that judges were more inclined to be lenient after a meal but more severe before the break.

***** This is because the stomach is competing with the brain and gets most of the blood sugar for digesting.

FINAL THOUGHTS

We could make sounds when we were about 9-14 months old. But it takes a long time to learn to communicate well as communication is not as simple as it seems to be on the surface. To accurately and efficiently transmit and exchange information, we need to carefully consider the other person's professional, psychological, and physiological needs in designing our messages and communication approach.

As leaders, we need to master the skills of optimizing our communication to achieve the best outcome. In summary, here are the three questions I ask myself before opening my mouth. I hope you can start trying the same:

- How could they interpret my words differently? (Lesson 1)
- Have I treated the interaction as a finite or an infinite game? (Lesson 2)
- What are the other person's needs? What can I do to address those needs in the communication?
    - Professional objectives (Lesson 3)
    - Psychological needs, such as being 'seen' (Lesson 4)
    - Physiological tendency to save brain energy (Lesson 5)

CHAPTER ENDNOTES

When I landed in the US in 2009, I knew my English was not so good. When I joined McKinsey in 2014, the need to improve communication was the most frequent feedback I got. I wish those who said, "Alice, you need to improve your communication," could have elaborated on what they meant. In 2021, I analyzed my struggles, deconstructed that vague feedback, and shared my lessons on leadership communication in this chapter.

Communication is hard. I don't know how you would interpret this chapter differently. The culture, situation, and specific problems you are facing will probably be different as well. You may not even have the same struggles as I had. However, I am sure we all want to be successful, be happy, or even leave a mark in the world. I hope this chapter will make it an easier journey for you to become an effective leader.

It is very likely that the chapter merely scratches the surface of the challenges you want to overcome. As someone who has experienced the continued need to adapt and learn from others, I am more than happy to be your companion along the infinite journey of improving ourselves to become successful leaders.

AUTHOR BIO

Alice Qinhua Zhou is a Senior Manager in EY's Financial Services Organization (FSO). As an executive in EY FSO's Profit Improvement practice, she advises senior executives from leading financial institutions on corporate and business unit strategy, efficiency improvement, and enterprise transformation. Prior to joining EY, she served Banking and Private Equity clients at McKinsey. She holds a Ph.D. degree in Computational Biophysics from Yale University and a B.S. degree in Biological Sciences from Fudan University in Shanghai, China.

Connect With Alice: Please feel free to contact me at FIRMSconsulting.com if you have any questions or comments.

CHAPTER 6

Facilitative Leadership for Posterity

BY AYLWIN SIM

MANY OF US are accustomed to the belief that leadership is all about your position in an organization. When someone is a senior executive, they have the privilege of leading those below them because they've reached a rank that we view as objectively superior. But is that really all there is to it?

Maybe once upon a time. In this day and age, however, mere rank isn't enough to make someone an effective leader. Rather, leadership is about learning how to get the most out of your employees through the ways in which you influence them. What does it mean to influence someone? At its core, it's about instilling a purpose to their actions. In my experience, this is the most important thing that there is. If you give someone a real reason for doing what they do, you've affected them far more than you could out of any straightforward act of authority.

Some people may tell you that a leader is supported by their team. While that may be true to some extent, my own time as a professional has shown me that, more often than not, the opposite is true: A team can only excel with the support of its leader.

GEMBA WALK

When you think of a leader in a corporate environment, how do you envision them? Do you imagine them interacting with their staff, conversing enthusiastically while they take stock of the daily operations in progress? Or do you picture someone seated behind a computer screen from nine to five in their secluded office, far removed from the menial frustrations of their subordinates' everyday activities?

If you find the second image to be more accurate, that makes sense. Many people calling themselves leaders will do exactly that sort of thing, day in and day out. However, these are the same people whose teams will consistently deliver mediocre or subpar performance. Truthfully, they aren't doing their jobs at all. These people aren't leaders. They're only supervisors.

Real leaders care about the state of their operations. They want to understand what's happening at every level, and they know that the only way to do that is by forging trust with their workers and examining processes firsthand. Oftentimes, the best way to do this is by physically putting oneself into the workplace and observing the ways in which it functions.

One Friday in April, just as I was packing up my work and preparing for the weekend, my manager, Ezra, requested a brief meeting. He asked me to investigate the operations and maintenance activities at a major wastewater treatment plant, which was managed by a local government council. I was excited to hear this, since it gave me an unprecedented opportunity to work closely with the operations team.

When I asked him what the issue was, his response was very telling: "Management has no visibility of where maintenance is being spent, and everything seems to be operating in a black box. We don't know why they needed capital investment, and there's an impression within the finance department that we might be gold-plating assets." He went on to say that the maintenance system they were running was entirely paper-based, operating primarily through index cards. This was the exact same way that the system had been run since the 1960s, when the plant was first constructed. Management, he explained to me, wanted maintenance at the treatment plant to be integrated into the current system. This was an enterprise resource planning system called SAP, which tracks costs while also optimizing the operations and maintenance of the plant and its equipment. By incorporating maintenance into SAP, my manager hoped to avoid the cost of upkeep that would be involved with implementing a new one.

The next week, I met with the plant manager, a man named Mark, and started asking questions about the operation of the plant. However, it soon became apparent that questions alone wouldn't be enough for me to garner a proper understanding of the issue at hand. Mark introduced me to his second in command, John, before showing me around the plant itself. As I was led through the eastern side of the building, illuminated by a spectacular sunrise, I began to work through the best way to consider and address the problem at hand.

I then decided that my best course of action was to walk the shop floor and meet the staff in order to ascertain the true nature of the problem. For about two weeks, I visited the plant every single day to talk with the staff and get a real sense of how the plant was operating, especially in regard to this odd little card system. This method of touring the shop floor is often referred to among manufacturers as a gemba walk. *Gemba*, which has no exact English equivalent, is a Japanese word that most succinctly translates to "the actual place." In this case, that actual place is the shop floor, where processes can be observed practically rather than theoretically. Frequent gemba walks are key to forging the connections and experiences that make for a successful leader.

Over this period of time, I learned that there was a lot more involved than the mere filing of index cards. The system operated like so: Each maintenance task was written on a single card. A specific pattern of holes was then physically punched into the top and side borders of each card, denoting the day, month, and year during which the task was meant to be performed. Once this was done, the cards would be stored in a red pinewood box, and subsequently retrieved with a metal rod on the corresponding day.

This was by all means a cleverly engineered system, but clearly not the most efficient option in our day and age. In addition to the obvious issues regarding lack of visibility, it also created an inability to analyze and optimize maintenance expenditure. While this seemed obvious to me, staff working within that environment had a different perspective. As far as they were concerned, things had always operated like this, and the system never caused them any egregious problems. If it ain't broke, why fix it, right?

This brought me to a crucial revelation. My task wasn't as straightforward as drawing up new processes and replacing the maintenance system entirely. In order for the changes to be effective, I would need to work not only with the management processes and the IT system, but also at the personnel level. If the engineers and technicians weren't onboard with my alterations, the whole thing was bound to crash and burn.

In order to ensure that the personnel were onboard with the change, therefore, I set aside a significant amount of time to convey our intentions and explain the benefits of transitioning to a digital system. I had Dave, an IT staff member, explain how the system would function, and ensured that they worked with the site technicians to implement the key training materials and standard operating procedures in the easiest way possible. He and I held presentations and demo sessions for everyone onsite with the full support of the management and team leaders.

Despite all of this, we still were met with resistance. In order to figure out the core issue, I had to dig a little deeper. Through doing so, I discovered that the majority of technicians who opposed the change were close to retirement. They weren't interested in the process of adopting new skills, since they would be out of the workforce in a matter of years, anyway. The younger technicians, on the other hand, were keen to start adopting the new system. I was able to identify that as our entry point for change.

One of these young technicians, Sam, told me that he wanted to stay relevant by always learning new skills. This gave me the idea to pair him up with an older technician and chose Dave for the job. Their partnership was incredibly effective: Sam was able to pick up the new skills he desired, while Dave could focus on training and knowledge transfer. Ultimately, Sam was able to use his freshly gained knowledge to help champion the change for us by getting his coworkers onboard. Inspired by Sam and David's success, we proceeded to pair up each younger technician with an older one, thereby enabling both groups to benefit from the change instead of opposing it.

The key to all of this was understanding Sam's individual motivation, and how it related to his group of peers. By walking the shop floor, one can get to know people on a human level, which in turn makes it possible to instill a sense of genuine purpose that serves as a driver for action and change.

The project turned out to be an absolute success. It helped the plant dodge unnecessary retrenchments, avoid decline in staff morale, and prevented the loss of years' worth of knowledge and experience, all while forming the foundation of a more centralized maintenance management system. Afterward, I was informed by Ezra and my mentor that they were surprised I had pulled off the transition. They previously tried to do so, they explained, by sending in a senior manager. That endeavor had been less effective: He was literally chased out of the plant and told not to set foot on the site again. I could see why they didn't elect to tell me that story before I got started on the project!

This entire experience solidified my belief that, as leaders, we can't overestimate the value of gemba walks. Only by engaging in this sort of activity can we comprehend the complexities of the challenges and issues that our staff are facing. Furthermore, it gives us the opportunity to acknowledge the good things that are happening, especially those that aren't mentioned in update reports. Another important lesson is that all change has a human side. When any sort of transformation occurs, people's lives will be affected, for better or for worse. Being cognizant about that is paramount to success. It isn't always easy, but there's no avoiding the fact that every story has a personal side. Acknowledging that and finding ways to accommodate it are the only ways to keep moving forward. The responsibility of a leader is to identify the primary lever that drives change. Usually, you'll find that it lies in the needs of your staff rather than your own.

If it's been a while since you last walked the shop floor, start making a habit of it. Connect with your staff. Be interested in the work that they're doing and take the time to listen to their concerns and challenges. Remember that your people are your assets, and that your company relies upon their well-being.

As leaders and managers, we don't like surprises. The same is true of our staff. When a change is going to be implemented, communicate and engage with them. Doing so is the key to success.

SYSTEMIC PROBLEM-SOLVING

One of the most important elements of leadership is understanding how to problem-solve. Before even beginning to think about fixing problems, however, it's worthwhile to take a minute to consider why problems exist in the first place.

If you view problems as irritating roadblocks or symptoms of systemic failure, you're going to have a lot of trouble maintaining confidence and success in your position of leadership. The truth is that, while they may be superficially undesirable, problems are inherent to the process of growth and improvement. If we never encountered any difficulties while pursuing our goals, then there would be no reason to be doing so in the first place. In fact, there's an argument to be made that even the word "problem" is an unfairly negative one. As a part of maintaining a more optimistic and productive mindset, I prefer to look at them as *opportunities*. However, the existence of an opportunity isn't enough to guarantee a beneficial development. It all depends on how you choose to address the issue at hand. It's essential to have a solid mindset from the outset: The right mindset will always drive the right action.

When confronting a problem, the first thing you need to do is take ownership. This doesn't mean that you should consider it to be entirely your own responsibility; relying on your team members to help you craft a solution is necessary more often than not. By "owning a problem," I mean that you need to acknowledge it fully and accept the fact that it will very likely have much deeper repercussions than you might anticipate or prefer. It's not an obstacle so much as it is a project. And, like any other project, it needs to be handled as something unique. If you're looking for a "one-size-fits-all" solution, you're essentially doing nothing more than slapping on a Band-Aid rather than addressing the core issue.

To approach a problem or opportunity in a truly effective manner, you'll need to deploy both linear and systemic methods of thinking. Let me explain what I mean by these terms. Linear thinking is a progression from cause to effect. When one issue is resolved, another related one will tend to pop up in its place. Linear thinking enables you to consider each of these problems in a vacuum so that you can thoroughly evaluate its distinct attributes. Systemic thinking, on the other hand, necessitates both breadth and depth to how you consider a problem. In other words, your initial approach to an issue should be backed by the understanding that it's likely the byproduct of another issue. Your priority becomes the mapping-out of linked occurrences in order to identify an underlying cause.

Once you've understood the systemic nature of a problem, the next step is to create a solution from the ground up. If all you do is aid the surface-level problems, it may be enough to repair the outstanding situation, but it won't transform the inner workings of your operation in a meaningful way. To create a lasting, impactful transformation, you need to involve every affected department. Envision yourself as an architect rather than a repairperson. You aren't just *fixing* a system that already exists; you're *building* something new.

At this point, recall the fact that you've taken ownership of the problem. While it's often helpful to solicit and consider input from other parties, your job isn't to seek out each and every individual with potential involvement in the issue. Instead, use your own knowledge—which, assuming that you've walked the shop floor and gotten to know your team members firsthand, should be easy—to work out who needs to be involved in your solution and in what ways.

Early in my consulting career, I was privileged with the opportunity to work with an electricity distribution company. I was asked to look at their governance in managing their core business. There are many sides to such review processes, as it's essential to see how every element relates to one another. These elements include how the company assesses future trends, how they operate and maintain their plant and equipment, how they deploy human resources, how they allocate financial capital to invest in new equipment, how they engage their customers, how they ensure that the best possible practices are captured and implemented within the company, and what training systems are implemented for the staff in order to keep them relevant within the market.

My client, whom I'll call Sean, mentioned that the company had recently undergone a major change in executives; all of them had been replaced within the last two to three years. Sean had only recently joined the company as a Chief Operating Officer, and even the CEO was new. The entire executive team had essentially been rebuilt.

My colleague and I went to visit our client first thing in the morning and proceeded to spend three full days learning the ins and outs of the situation. We conducted discussions with many of the new executives and staff to understand how they operated. Many of them expressed promising attributes: They were open to ideas, willing to work together, and generally imbued with positive energy. However, the majority of them were clearly still struggling to find their footing in their new positions. We were able to identify some areas of improvement such as silo-based thinking, but the main problems were a shortage of staff and overall lack of traction. These are common challenges that arise within such companies.

We eventually pinned down the main issue at hand: The company was missing its core purpose and had begun turning its attention toward areas of less relevance. Sean needed our help getting things back on track. At first, this was difficult to accept; it felt mundane, especially considering the rising interest in investing in new generation technologies–wind farms, solar farms, and so on. We were and still are, after all, moving toward a carbon free economy here in New Zealand. How could we go about realigning the company with its core values without coming across as limiting or recursive?

As we worked through workshops and interviews, we found that we had to change our approach. We began testing our observations regarding what qualified as core versus non-core business and started mixing personnel across different areas of operation and levels of seniority. At one point, we were in conversation with a senior manager in HR, the GM of community services, and management staff from engineering, all in one group. While we worked through the issues at hand, the HR manager began to realize that changes to the engineering side of things actually had an effect on HR and how the company communicated its progress to the community.

For example, we identified a need to upgrade skills and track staff development to support engineering. The engineering staff then realized in turn that there was a constraint in the hiring process and that the company needed to do a better job of communicating its progress to the community and getting it involved in its decision-making. Siobhan, the HR manager, said that it was eye-opening, further explaining, "I didn't realize there was a lot of impact from engineering to HR and back that's involved in managing our core business." Jasper from Communications suggested that, "By involving our communities in our decision-making process, we can better focus our investments; after all, they are our stakeholders."

With these findings in mind, we reported back to Thomas, the CEO. He was a great listener with a pleasant personality. With our guidance, he began to refocus the company with an emphasis on solidifying the need for proper governance within the core business. Sean eagerly began working with his peers to put the new systems and processes in place. Things were finally starting to move in the right direction.

When faced with a problem in your workplace, try adjusting your perspective to think not only bigger, but also deeper. Seek out perspectives across myriad areas and levels of seniority in order to employ a robust decision-making process that changes not only the way people work, but the way people think. Study the ways in which you may be able to use this opportunity to your advantage and improve the core culture of your company. We'll talk about dynamism within business culture later in this chapter, but for now, let's turn our gazes inward, at our own personal journeys.

WORKS IN PROGRESS

All of us are works in progress. Nobody ever finishes the process of self-improvement. With this in mind, it may be more effective to think of us not as fully formed leaders, but rather as leaders in the making. Every day, we need to get up with the intention of bettering ourselves, while simultaneously bringing out the best in others.

During the Canterbury and Christchurch earthquakes from 2010 to 2011, I was a recent business school graduate. The first major quake struck New Zealand's South Island at 4:35 a.m. on September 4th. It registered at a 7.1 on the Richter scale. Aftershocks followed shortly after; the strongest being on February 22nd, with a 6.3 shock near Christchurch. This was much more destructive than the initial impact, resulting in 185 deaths. According to Deloitte, the damage bill racked up to 40 billion dollars, making it the fifth-biggest insurance event in the world since 1953.

The standard protocol in the event of an earthquake was to make sure that our family and close ones were safe before reporting for civil defense duty. At the time, my manager, Bruce, was away in Europe on vacation. I managed to get in contact with his manager, Scott, who asked me to come into the office; we needed all the help we could get.

Around 8:00 a.m., I made my way to a temporary office, since our usual location was under structural assessment. Eventually, Scott let me know that the main office was compromised, and we wouldn't be able to use it at all. As I drove down the road, I didn't see much damage in the area. Approaching the city, however, felt like entering a ghost town. It was completely deserted. Cracks ran through the buildings and roads. We traveled farther north, only to discover even worse damage: burst water pipes, damaged bridges, land sliding into rivers... It looked like the end of the world.

There are three phases involved in managing a disaster. The first is civil defense, in which we ensure the safety of the buildings and infrastructure around us. This means that any buildings deemed unrecoverable would be marked for demolition. The second phase, operating in parallel, is recovery. This consists of the gathering and analysis of as much information as possible in order to begin preparing for the final phase: rebuilding.

At 10:00 a.m., I was asked to attend a meeting with senior managers. I was instructed to lead a team to pull together all the information we could gather on the state of infrastructure, particularly underground assets such as water and wastewater pipes. These are critical during a disaster and can lead to a health crisis if left unaddressed. We also needed to show the progress that we were making in terms of repairs and keep the public informed in order to avoid any civil unrest.

For context, I was in a junior role when I was asked to lead a team to resolve this issue. The purpose was clear, but only two other colleagues of mine understood the systems and processes that had recently been implemented after the centralization of our management systems. One of them, Trevor, was in the northern hemisphere on vacation, set to return in three to four days. Another, Leanne, was in the vicinity. I called her, and she came immediately. Still, we needed an extra team member to work on geospatial mapping. This role was crucial in order to ensure that we could display the data on a visual map. Without it, we wouldn't be able to target our repairs. Worse than that, we couldn't show our progress to the public, which could result in a health crisis.

I was personally capable of taking on the role. However, it would be better in the long run if we could get someone to work with the software and convert the datasets so that I could focus on clearing the way for my team to operate as effectively as possible. Getting the right people on the bus was the key step. It's always important to find others who have better technical skills to supplement your performance team.

With my requirements prepared, my first point of contact would be the geospatial department. I met in person with Jessica, the team leader, to present our needs. I tried to emphasize the importance of supporting us in providing information to support engineering and keep the public up to date. Her response was that they were short on personnel, and therefore unable to allocate resources. Despite the fact that she claimed to be tied up doing similar things with buildings and properties, I continually checked in with them for resources. We eventually managed to get support from them during the second major earthquake on February 22nd, but that's a story for another time.

A few days after my discussion with the geospatial team, I got a call from a graduate engineer named Heather offering to provide help. In a case of wonderful serendipity, it just so happened that a manager was trying to deploy additional resources and found that my team was in need of support. She came in first thing in the morning and got right to work, managing to reduce the turnaround period on the maps from five days to one. This was a significant improvement to what we were used to, even prior to the earthquake. The management team was delighted with the output and commended us for our effort. Moving forward, our focus shifted toward ensuring that our data was of the highest possible quality.

There are three things that I want senior leaders to learn from this story. Firstly, you will inevitably be put in situations outside of our comfort zone. Look at this as an opportunity to grow and implement your personal method of doing things. Secondly, when building a team, surround yourself with people who are experts in their function. Everybody has different strengths, and it's the responsibility of the leader to capitalize upon them. Thirdly, create a culture that cultivates and appreciates the people around you. You should view your role as a way to help others reach their full potential.

Throughout this entire experience, I suffered from no small amount of self-doubt. What had I signed up for? I knew what I wanted to accomplish, but how was I going to pull it off? Where would I find the people that would help me do so? At that point, I was reminded of something that my mentor said to me a few years back: "All the education, work experience, and training that we receive is to prepare us to manage a disaster." If we can maintain confidence in a worst-case scenario, we've done our jobs well.

Treat everything as an opportunity to better yourself. As my mentor described, everything in life serves as a preparation for us to take on something seemingly insurmountable. Our work is bigger than ourselves. When we operate as a team, we do so for the greater good of society. We only get to live life once; make it count!

PAYING ATTENTION TO CULTURE

Peter Drucker once said that culture eats strategy for breakfast. A lot of people assume that strategy is the most important element of successful business. While its value certainly shouldn't be underestimated, culture is equally essential. Only in the right culture can strategies be executed successfully.

After the earthquakes of 2010 and 2011, I was asked to join a power company. The company was currently preparing for an IPO, in which the government would divest 49% of its shareholding to the public.

The issue at hand was the lack of an investment plan. Such a plan would show how the company invested capital in order to maintain, renew, and upgrade its power generation assets. Without a clear plan in line to cover corporate strategy and risk, the company ran the risk of overinvesting in maintenance, thereby failing to optimize investments throughout the company as a whole.

So it was that I found myself occupying a senior position in a new industry. I presented my approach to the management team, whom I needed onboard in order to access their team members. I began this presentation by asking a question: "On a scale of one to ten, where do we see ourselves in the process of implementing this change?" A 'one' would indicate that we were *talking* the talk, while a 'ten' meant we were *walking* the walk. "At least we should be a seven, if not an eight," one manager noted, and the rest of the room nodded their agreement. The General Manager then declared that, "We need to be at least at an eight," which was enough to assure me that they were fully invested in this journey.

As a newcomer, it was crucial for me to understand how the company operated, as well as the direction in which it was headed. Getting commitment from the managers was also essential. The core team that I needed for this engagement was a cross-functional one, composed of personnel from engineering, finance, operations, and trading. A cross-functional team like this allows for the opportunity to obtain insights that we can't see from the confines of our own functional expertise. It also provides a chance to break down any silos that may be emerging within the company.

While working on the project, we were able to pull together the information that we needed in order to prepare the investment plans for each power station. However, I quickly realized that the underlying culture of the operations department was focused on keeping the lights on. Their capital budgets were capped by finance because the investments were not sufficiently justified, and the risks were not well-understood.

The deployment of a cross-functional team was part of the solution, but we also needed a cultural shift in the operations department. By creating a shift in the way that operations thought about capital and expenditure in relation to the company's strategy and risk profile, we could create an opportunity in which better business cases would be approved, while also ensuring that the decision makers fully understood the trade-off between investment and risk that would be involved in making such a decision. Since the responsibility of decision-making falls on the executive team and board of directors, this was especially crucial.

My main takeaway from this experience was that culture is just as important as strategy. When we want to implement a solution, we need to consider the current culture of the organization in comparison to what the new culture needs to be and identify the interventions necessary to get from one to another. These interventions vary depending on the situation. They might involve restructuring, weekly communications in newsletters, or all sorts of other methods. The most important thing is that the leadership keeps communicating and puts processes in place that will help to drive the new culture.

Having the right people on the team is also essential. In this case, there was a need for a cross-functional team so that various experts could provide advice on what needed to be done from their own perspectives. As leaders, we should always surround ourselves with people who are smarter than us in their technical field. We also need to make sure that we're asking the right questions so that we can conduct an informed discussion.

Lastly, this experience taught me that there are times in which opportunities find us. Leaders need to be open to those opportunities. They tend to be unique, meaning that we won't repeat our same duties every day for 10 years. Instead, we should actively learn and engage. Every year or two, we need to take on new challenges and opportunities that will push us to the next level of success.

FINAL THOUGHTS

Leadership is a work in progress, an endless process of self-discovery. It's a journey that we take to understand who we are as people. We constantly seek to improve ourselves and those around us while also bringing the best of what we are. It all starts with us seeing ourselves as leaders and refusing to sell ourselves short.

We also need to realize that everything will fall into place given time. When we look back and reflect upon our experiences, it's easy to find milestones and anchor experiences that have shaped us and our thinking, even if we didn't recognize them while they were happening. Self-reflection like this enables us to move onto the next level in our personal leadership journey. Still, we can't only rely on our experiences, or we risk getting trapped in the past. Rather, we need to acknowledge what we've been through while also moving on to experience new things in life.

A greater implication of this is that you'll often find that you need to detach yourself from end goals. The process of discovery is an infinite one, and the best thing that you can do is make use of the time that you have to achieve, adapt, and grow as much as possible. Know and remember that there is always a better version of yourself, and if you continue to pursue it, you'll accomplish more than you ever could have imagined.

This doesn't mean that you're guaranteed riches, fame, or outstanding career success. Not everyone can be president, after all; but everyone *can* be the best version of themselves. Focus on your own capabilities and ambitions. Don't try to be everything at once. Find your niche, and pursue the best ways to fulfill, redefine, and expand it. This can be daunting, but don't be discouraged. All of us are intimidated by the unknown. It's only in retrospect that we can see how all the pieces have fallen into place. Remember that you've gotten this far by doing the right thing and challenge yourself to see how much more you can achieve.

While on this journey, we must continually improve ourselves, but that's not all. We also need to focus on nurturing the next generation of leaders. Think of a parent raising a child: They want the best for their children and even hope that their children can accomplish even more than they have themselves. Your purpose as a leader is to provide the type of guidance that will make this possible for your own peers and mentees. Keep in mind that the people learning from you will often fail and maintain enough humility to remember that you were once in the same position as them. We can't prevent others from making mistakes entirely, but we *can* use our own experiences to steer them in the right direction, and to teach them how to pick themselves back up after they fall down.

We aren't here to earn positions and titles. Those are short-lived and ultimately do the world no good. Instead, we're here to bring out the best in others and facilitate a brighter future for humanity.

AUTHOR BIO

Aylwin Sim is a management consultant with extensive experience in asset intensive organizations, governance, operations strategy, and implementation. He advises executives of growth-oriented companies to maximize their investments of time, money and talent toward what will make the biggest impact on their growth and change initiatives. He holds an MBA and a bachelor's degree in engineering from University of Canterbury in New Zealand. Aylwin is a business professional with a decades-long track record of successfully implementing and executing strategy in the corporate and government environment. He believes in the value of company culture and works alongside staff across all company sects and levels of seniority in order to ensure that systemic changes are as deep-rooted and effective as possible. Through continual acts of exploration and improvement for both himself and his companies, he aspires to leave a sustainable impact that shapes a better future for everyone involved.

CHAPTER 7

Leadership Through Financial Management

BY TAKAHIRO AJIMIZU

THERE ARE MANY PEOPLE who want to be leaders in business: some people succeed, others don't. On the contrary, there are those who are reluctant to be leaders but succeed, nonetheless. Are there any common factors that cultivate successful leadership? My answer is, "Yes and no."

As the most basic thing, expressing your intention or will to become a leader is very important. However, at the same time, it is also important to realize that you cannot be a leader by yourself. The support of people around you and your superiors is essential.

Therefore, it is ideal to both express your intention and be recognized as a leader by others. You know, however, that it doesn't really work that simply because business involves political and economic factors, such as interests.

Also, becoming a true leader who is worshiped is not something that can be easily achieved, but is developed from the natural recognition by others by continuing to exercise your leadership. It's easy to imagine that if you don't have the qualities of a leader by nature, it will take a lot of effort and time to be respected.

The reason I first answered 'yes' and 'no' is that I think the answer depends on the person and the circumstances around them. As a leader, you should have your own rules and attitudes, but it's also a problem to be bound by stereotypes.

I don't think of myself as a great leader, so in this chapter, I'd like to touch on my leadership expertise that is closer to management and that anyone should be able to practice.

I am currently a consultant, but I have worked for a company that hires consultants as a client. Therefore, it is possible to write my experiences from both perspectives so that the content is valuable to both client companies and consultants.

Since we, as consultants, have a duty of confidentiality, we cannot quote actual experiences to protect our clients and workplaces. Please understand that in this chapter, I demonstrate my leadership based on a fictitious story.

I'm also a member of FIRMSconsulting, the publisher of this book. So, I explain leadership by incorporating the strategic techniques of FIRMSconsulting in addition to the insights gained from my experiences. By doing so, it is possible to introduce the work more efficiently and effectively.

I not only think anyone has the potential to become a successful leader, but also that they *should* be in some capacity. As a concept, I want to make this chapter what I wanted to read when I was in my 20s.

LEADERSHIP THEORIES WITH INSIGHTS

Before I dive into the details, let's talk about my leadership theories with some insights. Based on the theories, I will subsequently introduce a case study in a form close to actual business engagement.

The reason why I present the information in this way is that, when I was young, I had a separate understanding of the overall strategic work and the work of financial analysts. As a result, there were times when the content of the report did not connect as a story. No one was around to systematically explain strategy and finance as a whole at that time. Therefore, I found it worthwhile to introduce some of my methods here.

I believe this format reinforces leadership through financial strategy.

DEFINITION

Firstly, I would like to define the term 'Leadership.' What is leadership in the first place?

Is a leader an influential person, such as making people dream, changing the mindset of others, or guiding people? Is a leader a person who stands on top of others? Is a leader a person who directs people? It seems that people have different ideas. Leadership and management are often confused. So, let's clarify here.

According to Wikipedia, "Leadership means that an individual, group, or organization with humanity and practical skills leads, influences, or guides an individual, team, or organization."

Management, however, is defined as "the administration of an organization that includes the activities of setting the strategy of an organization and coordinating the efforts of its employees to accomplish its objectives through the application of available resources, such as financial, natural, technological, and human resources."

As you can see, the "practical skills" described in the definition of leadership are considered to refer to 'management.' In other words, leadership encompasses management skills.

Moreover, leadership is not just important for teams and organizations. You can exercise it between individuals, and even within, to motivate and guide oneself. Clients assess your leadership capabilities by observing not only how you manage other people, but also how you manage yourself. In general, leadership tends to emphasize how to guide others. Focusing solely on teamwork-leadership can diminish the behavior of some members and undermine individual opinions and ideas.

I believe that leadership begins with personal practice. And being recognized as a leader through practice, gives you an influential position to guide your team or organization. In other words, it is necessary to have the ability as a leader from the beginning, and I think that there are many people who stumble for that reason.

When I was working for a client-side company, a few consultants tried to become project leaders without knowing much about our jobs and needs. As a result, the project was different from the original plan and was confusing. Even if it makes money, a good leader should not accept a job that cannot be done. The profession of consultant is suitable for people who empathize with others and like helping them. This is because it is a job that supports the business of others.

The importance of exercising leadership for oneself is often underestimated, so in this chapter, I would like to discuss basic leadership primarily for individuals. I sincerely hope that many will gain invaluable insights.

LEADERSHIP CATEGORIES

Secondly, there are many types of leaders in the world. Since the purpose is not to analyze and classify leaders academically, I will generalize and summarize them.

I would like to divide leadership into four quadrants based on my experiences. Please imagine that "Top-Down" and "Bottom-Up" are listed as leadership approaches on one axis. On the other axis, the character of the leader is described as a "Logical Thinker" and an "Intuitive Thinker."

Top-down leaders generally have a strong personality that is admired by people and tend to be extremely valued, for better or for worse. They have the strengths to attract and guide people by showing a vision or strategy that draws attention with a passionate presentation. A typical example is Steve Jobs, the founder of Apple Inc.

Bottom-up leaders, on the other hand, generally have a soft personality that is respected by people and tend to be rated moderately. They value the work in the field and have the strengths to attract and motivate people so that employees can make their own decisions and work responsibly. It can be said that bottom-up leadership creates many leaders under the leader. A typical example here is Stephen Wozniak, another founder of the same Apple company.

Steve and Stephen are both great leaders, but they are completely different types. The success of Apple companies today is believed to be due to the synergistic effects of their strengths.

It's important to know in which quadrant you and your clients are located. For example, I practice bottom-up leadership and my thinking is intuitive in nature, but I have trained and learned logical thinking. Therefore, I have the approach and character that it is more likely to be favored by top-down and intuitive leaders. This is because I think it is easy to build positive relationships that complement each other in terms of personality and ability.

There is no right or wrong answer, so please find your best leadership practice by considering your personality, temperament, strengths, and weaknesses.

FIND LEADERS YOU RESPECT

Thirdly, do you have someone you admire in your life and business? If you have such a person, they will be mentally helpful for being able to do your best without giving up when faced with difficulties. I would like to introduce three people that I respect as a guideline for my life.

The first person is Tsugunosuke Kawai, a great leader and strategist: "Tsugunosuke Kawai (January 27, 1827–October 1, 1868) was a Japanese samurai of the late Edo period, who served the Makino clan of Nagaoka. Kawai was a senior military commander of Nagaoka forces during the Boshin War of 1868–1869."

He is said to have led people with strong leadership and fought many times more enemies with good strategy and the latest weapons of the time, such as the Gatling gun.

The second person is Wang Yang-ming of China who Kawai worshiped, an excellent military strategist and philosopher who was described as having fought with a sword in his right hand and a book in his left hand. It is said that his teachings had a huge influence on both the government army and samurai during the Meiji Restoration in Japan.

Given the number of pages, it is difficult to explain their teachings in simple terms, so to name a similar person and philosophy in the West, Friedrich Nietzsche and his philosophy "Will to Power" as well as "Eternal Recurrence" are likely to be close—at least I found many similarities. He is the third person; I think everyone has heard the name at least once.

My philosophy of life and principles of action are greatly influenced by Kawai, Yang-ming, and Nietzsche.

ACCURATE, HIGH-QUALITY WORK

Next, let's think about the leaders we are generally looking for. We want good leaders to do the work we expect and get results at a higher level. At the very least, the leader needs to make sure that they get the job done as expected from clients or team members. It sounds obvious, but I write it because even good leaders sometimes forget about it.

For example, if you order a steak at a restaurant, you want to eat a delicious steak. Even if a delicious side dish or dessert comes out, you will be dissatisfied if the main meal is not tasty. Business is the same. We tend to overlook the fact that what we think is good and what our customers and team members expect, may be different. Before you take on a job or work as a team together, it is very important to make sure that expectations are met.

NUMBERS ARE UNIVERSAL FINANCIAL LANGUAGE

Next, what I notice through working with various people is that knowing the figures is the beginning of everything. Unlike languages, everyone can understand numbers and they are an international financial language.

Ideas that create business value leverage creativity that is difficult to quantify, but ultimately sales, profits, assets, liabilities, stock prices, cash flow, etc. are all represented by numbers. Therefore, business consultants should at least provide service or value that can be converted into figures as deliverables.

In a corona pandemic world where face-to-face communication is restricted, numerical communication becomes especially important.

HAVE STRENGTHS IN TECHNOLOGY, INVESTMENT, AND FINANCE

Current leaders need to have strengths in each of all three categories: technology, investment, and finance.

In this chapter, for example, technology, knowledge of IT, agriculture, and electronics will occupy a large volume in the next case study. In investment, it is required to recognize and understand the importance of capital expenditure. When it comes to finance, raising equity capital and subsidies is essential.

As you may have noticed, it's the same idea as the cash flow statement. Corporate technology with competitive advantage generates operating cash flow, which is used to make capital investments (i.e., investing cash flow), and the shortfall is covered by financing cash flow.

I feel that financial knowledge is crucial not only at the corporate level but also at the small business or individual level. Therefore, I would like to introduce an overview of how I comprehensively utilize technology, investment, and finance knowledge in decision-making as a leader using financial models and analysis later.

LEADERSHIP IS BOTH ART AND SCIENCE

In the previous sections, I mentioned the importance of knowing the financial figures of a business. That is science. With that in mind, leaders also need an artistic sensibility. It may be possible to paraphrase art as intuition and sensibility and science as logic and rationality.

Successful CEOs (Chief Executive Officers) or presidents usually have great intuition or creativity that creates new value. As numerical analysis and forecasting models are sometimes built on historical data, it cannot be used as a reference when society is undergoing major changes such as the corona pandemic. Besides, top leaders often make quick decisions on a monthly or daily basis and may not have time to wait for the results of the analysis created by financial analysts. In such cases, intuition or creativity is ultimately the deciding factor.

On the other hand, middle managers and field managers need to have a good balance of both scientific knowledge and artistic sensibility. In order for people to understand their thoughts, it is important to create an interesting story and show it logically with figures.

In this chapter, I would like to mainly discuss leadership for middle managers and field managers. There are two reasons for this: First, I infer most of the readers of this book are corporate employees and second, I think the intuitive and creative abilities required of CEOs and presidents have a large innate element. If they have innate talents, it will be difficult to imitate.

LEADERSHIP CAN BE LEARNED THROUGH VARIOUS EXPERIENCES

Finally, I have worked in the agricultural industry for several years. It has provided very meaningful experiences because I could learn a wide range of fields. Agriculture is built on deep relationships with people, nature, and animals, so it has much in common with business.

For example, before you grow a crop, you need to know the appropriate environmental conditions for that crop. Next, you need to make sure that the location you choose is suitable for growth. This is like human resource management work.

And then, you buy seeds or seedlings. You need to exercise caution when choosing the seedlings to plant. This is because the quality of seedlings has a great influence on the prognosis of growth. On the business side, this is the equivalent of an interview to hire talented people.

During cultivation, various factors such as sunlight, carbon dioxide, water, fertilizer, soil, and air volume affect growth. It doesn't just grow with water and fertilizer. How much sunlight, water, and fertilizer you need depends entirely on the plant. The same is true for people. We learn and grow from various experiences.

Furthermore, there is a deep philosophical correlation with the fact that plant roots continue to grow underground in cold weather and when it gets warmer, the expanded roots are used to grow branches and leaves to bear fruit. This plant growth process provides implications for decision-making and business life cycle thinking.

The concept of time is also important. No matter how good the growing environment and conditions are, it will take a certain period to harvest. The growth of a person is the same. It takes time for a person to grow physically and mentally.

The point here is that if your career so far is not directly related to leadership or management, don't give up. Your past work experiences can give you a competitive advantage that cannot be easily imitated by others. We can learn a lot from various work experiences; your value depends on how you see things.

Now, it is the time to show you how I have practiced leadership based on these theories and insights. Clients always want to know, "So what?" and "So how?" Please keep these questions in mind while you read the case study.

LEADERSHIP CASE STUDY

In this section, I will show my leadership practices in a chronological format.

As explained previously, my exact past experiences cannot be disclosed due to confidentiality obligations, but the insights given in this story are based on actual experiences.

Specific numbers shown here, such as assumptions, are for reference only. Prerequisites of this project can vary by country and location, so if you would like to refer to this content for your own business, please check the environment and conditions of your country, such as laws, natural environment, suppliers, subsidy, etc.

To make the content even more effective, I would like to introduce some of the strategic techniques of FIRMSconsulting. If you would like to know more, please visit their website.

The case study covers leadership, management, and strategy, with some reference to financial models and analytics that are important in decision-making. The industries involved are e-commerce in the field of IT, tourism, and agriculture that incorporates environmental control technology.

For strategists, ingenuity and creativity are important, and there is not always a fixed method. However, things are a little different for consultants who support the business of others. Logic and science may be more important, as it makes no sense unless the value of the deliverable is properly communicated to the client.

For financial analysts, there are certain rules that should be followed. It is important, as a professional, to be able to demonstrate some ingenuity and creativity under established financial rules.

Strategists and financial analysts require different abilities and skills. It's no wonder that many large consulting firms work in teams of members with different expertise.

But this chapter focuses on individual leadership, not teams. This is because individual leadership is a prerequisite for demonstrating team leadership, and I believe it is more beneficial to highlight.

By covering a wide range of fields, I will endeavor to make the content interesting to as many people as possible.

PHASE 0: BEFORE FORMAL ENGAGEMENT

This phase, which is before officially taking on the job from a client, is the most important part for me as a professional.

Some of you may feel that I think too much before starting, but please keep in mind that the quality of work depends on how much time you spend on preparation.

The right questions are needed to get the right answers quickly in the client's limited time and budget, and some prior information and analysis is needed to ask the right questions.

The work of the consultant after Phase 1 can often be seen by clients, but since the work of Phase 0 is usually before receiving the request, clients may not have a chance to see it. Therefore, it may be valuable, in a sense, to know what a strategic consultant thinks behind the scenes.

By the way, all important information exchanges and confirmations are done by email in my case. This is because they are recorded as text. It gives me most of the information I need for analysis, so preparing Phase 0 questions and analytics is usually not a problem.

Some clients suggest meeting first. But please remember that there is no free lunch in business. As long as labor costs are incurred, it will always be reflected in the price in some way. Considering cost-effectiveness or return on investment, it is difficult to judge whether it is worth it. If the client thinks mutual trust is important, it's a good idea to build trust little by little through small jobs first.

If we don't take enough time to prepare and think about the problems we are hired to solve, it is difficult to produce insightful deliverables. I think it is no exaggeration to say that 50% of success is decided here. This is very important for me at least.

First Contact From Client

First, let's explain the background of the request from the client so that the overall story flow is easy to understand.

One day a prospect, Fred, who is the CEO of Gorgeous Fruits Inc. in the United States, contacted me because he wanted to start a strawberry picking business. I was wondering why he thought that way, so I asked him. He said that he had experienced the strawberry picking service when he traveled to Japan, and he was very satisfied and enjoyed it. Therefore, he wanted to provide a similar service locally.

Since I was involved in the agricultural industry, I also knew that Japanese sweet strawberries were popular with foreign tourists. Given the potential demand overseas, I thought it could be a good business opportunity. Another reason for starting a business in the United States was that the corona pandemic made it difficult to travel abroad.

With just a little thought, some considerations that came up are mapped out in Exhibit 1. There were additional considerations since the request was from overseas.

EXHIBIT 1: *Consideration of Request*

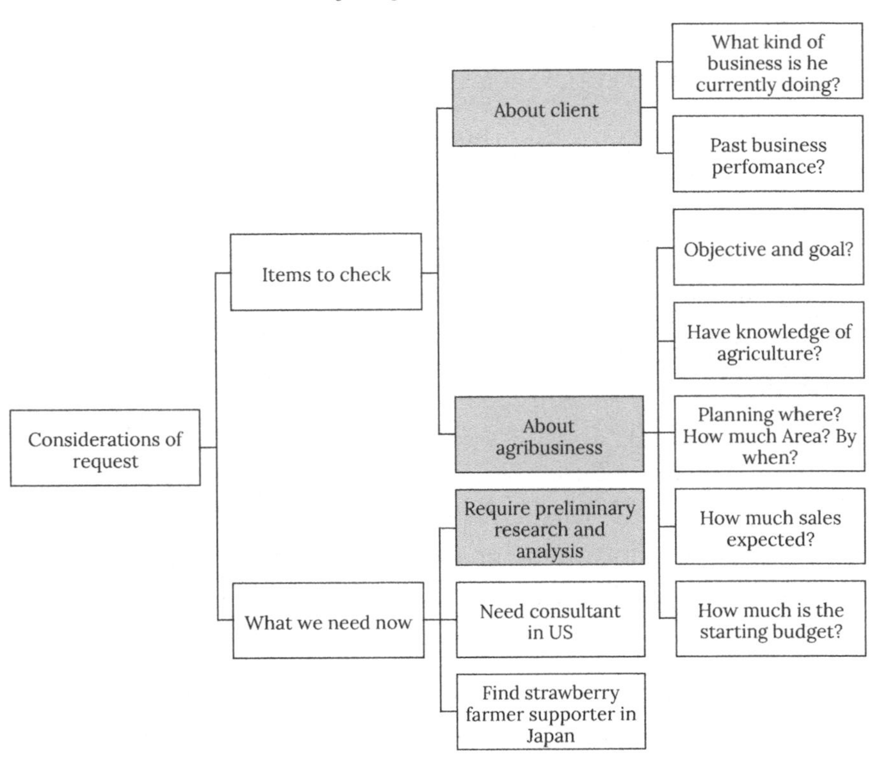

Please note that at this stage, I hadn't been formally commissioned to work yet, but I called Fred a client.

First Consultant Reply to Client

All the above considerations are important, but let's prioritize them.

It was unclear if I could provide enough value for my client, so I needed to do some preliminary research and analysis first. I also prepared an estimate for payment.

When I replied to client Fred, I informed him in advance that preliminary research and analysis would be required and that it costs a little. Fees vary depending on how far the pre-research and analysis is conducted, but I try to keep it to the minimum necessary to determine future policies.

As a side note, if you are a business consultant and don't have the specific business expertise that your client is involved in, don't worry too much. The information you need as a consultant can often be obtained more accurately from client interviews and financial analysis later. Unless the client is looking for operational knowledge and skills for a specific field, you can leverage your strengths as a business professional.

It is also quite beneficial for client companies to pay for the preliminary research and analysis in this early stage. There are three reasons for this:

1. The early strategy planning has a great impact on the quality of consulting service later.
2. A client can understand what they are paying for.
3. As long as a client makes a payment each time, it is less likely to be a problem no matter when/if they cancel their request.

It is important for strategic leaders to be aware of how to receive payment properly for services, so I explained here—think flexibly according to the client's request and conditions.

First Client Reply to Consultant:

Dear Takahiro,

Thank you for your reply. I want to answer the questions you sent the other day.

I have been running an e-commerce site since 2017 that sells various expensive and valuable fruits. Sales and profits are summarized in the attached materials. Since the corona pandemic, online sales have skyrocketed due to the spread of home-based work.

I'm interested in a strawberry picking start-up business, but I have no experience in agriculture. So, if you know of a Japanese strawberry picking firm that could provide me some advice, I would appreciate it if you could let me know.

The aim is to build a greenhouse on a hectare of land and launch a profitable strawberry picking service as early as possible in the United States. The goal is to have many people enjoy strawberry picking.

I can't imagine the budget, but it would be great if I could keep it low. I will utilize subsidy if available. I'm thinking of a location near Seattle, Washington.

Certainly, I think it would be easier for me to consult if there is one experienced consultant in the United States. If you know anyone, please let me know.

Finally, regarding the payment of costs for preliminary research and analysis, can you tell us what the report includes and how much it will cost?

Regards,

Fred -----------

Chief Executive Officer

Gorgeous Fruits Inc.

http://-----------------.com

Insights Gained at This Stage

You can get some insights from the client's response. For example, it seems that the client's interest in the new business is not only because he was satisfied with the strawberry picking experience in Japan, but also because the sales of e-commerce business have increased rapidly in the last few years. From data such as sales and profits, it is possible to infer how the client's business is faring and whether he can afford to invest in a new business. Also, considering that the client is already in the e-commerce business, he may be considering the synergistic effect of combining different businesses.

Objectives of Creating a Preliminary Report

Preparation of a preliminary report has several purposes. Here, I will explain them from the perspective of a consultant.

First, check if there is any difference in information or thinking between the client and the consultant. And since I didn't know the size of the client's budget, I thought it was important to first give a rough idea of how much sales would be generated and the initial investment that would be required. That information then prompts the client to decide what to do next.

A detailed competitor research and analysis was not conducted in this case study. There are two reasons: One is that I am not familiar with the US market, and the other is that research using paid databases is not realistic at this request scale. Many are assumed to be small and medium-sized competitors and are considered private companies that are not publicly traded. It is unlikely that I would get useful information from paid service as a benchmark.

If the client understood the work of the consultant, and I performed the appropriate research and analysis at the right time, it would be much easier to provide high-value services at an affordable price as a result.

Creating Charter for Preliminary Report

Before preparing the preliminary report, I created a charter to summarize the client's request to know the contents of the preliminary research and analysis. A charter is a 'promise' or 'contract' that confirms and is agreed on with clients and teams before work begins. It organizes commitments in terms of objectives, scope of work, key activities, deliverables, and critical success factors. More information about charters can be found in the FIRMSconsulting book *The Strategy Journal* by Kris Safarova.

EXHIBIT 2: *Preliminary Research and Analysis Charter*

<table>
<tr><th>Objectives</th><th>Key Activities</th><th>Deliverables</th></tr>
<tr><td>• Determine minimum requirements for success and confirm they are met
• Estimate the fee for preliminary research and analysis
• Decide on whether to proceed the business planning</td><td rowspan="3">• Expectation exchange with client/consultant to agree on deliverables
• Develop key question (if the objective is clear at this point)
• Structure, estimate and hypothesize for the study and get buy-in
• Identify key issues required to run detailed analysis later
• Approach to consultants (to find prospective team member) in US
• Approach to prospective farmers who can support in Japan
• Assist client in developing decision-making criteria</td><td>a) Workflow diagram
b) Current e-commerce business
• Business model diagram
• Profitability framework diagram
c) New strawberry picking business
• Business model diagram
d) Preliminary estimation excerpts
• E-commerce top-down estimation
• Strawberry top-down estimation
• Initial capital investment estimation
e) Others
• Hypotheses and insights
• Future human resource proposals</td></tr>
<tr><th>Scope</th><th>Critical Success Factors</th></tr>
<tr><td>• Top-Down or market demand approach estimation
• Only in Seattle or surroundings, Washington, USA
• Only in e-commerce as well as in strawberry industry</td><td>• Timely access to information
• Both client and consultant commitment
• Clear, open, and honest communication
• Accurate data</td></tr>
</table>

Once the client was satisfied with the charter (or conditions) above, and the payment for the preliminary investigation was confirmed, I started preparing the report.

First Deliverables to the Client

The following is an excerpt of the contents of the report:

- Workflow diagram overview
    - As a result of considering the content of the client's initial consultation, I suggested that we work according to the following schedule.

EXHIBIT 3: *Workflow Diagram*

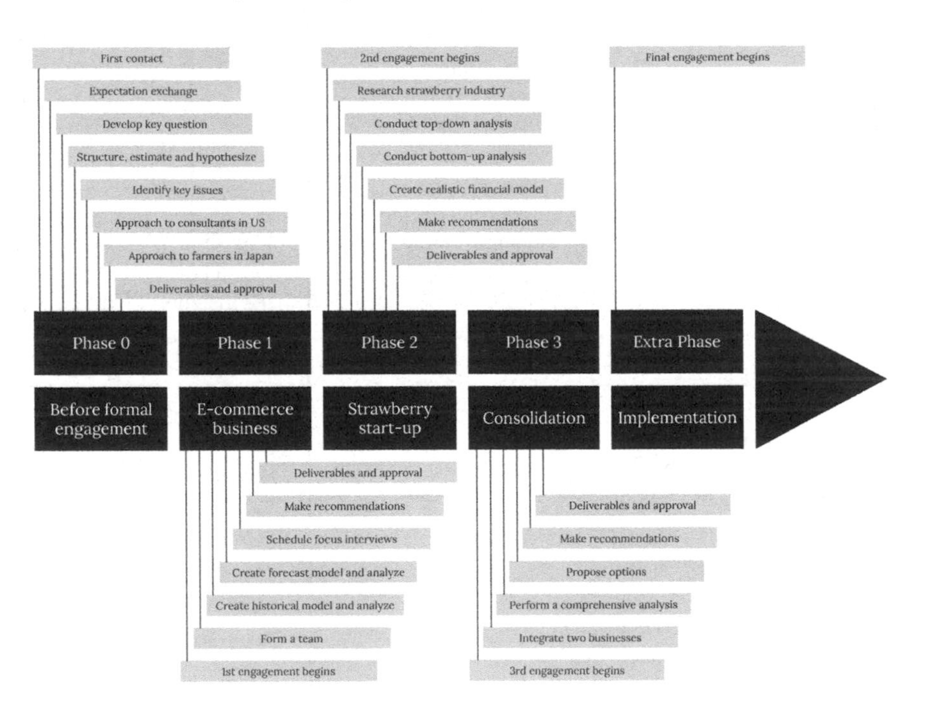

- Current e-commerce business
  - This is the client's e-commerce business model diagram created based on the received information.

EXHIBIT 4: *E-Commerce Business Model*

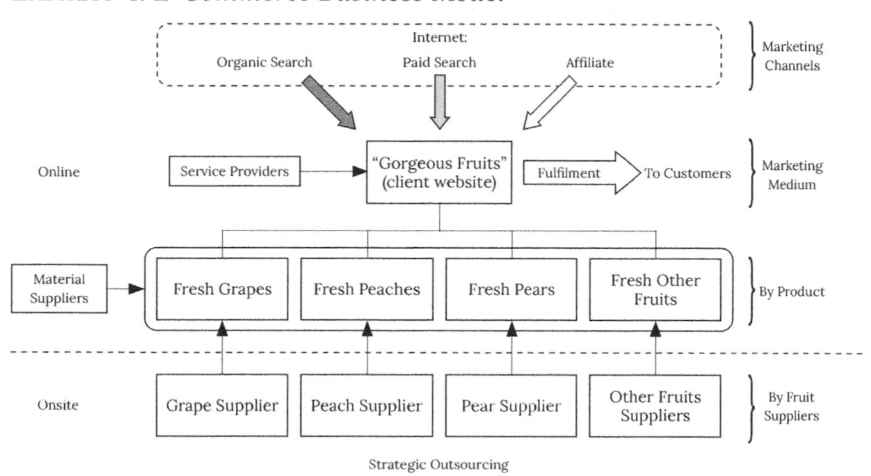

This diagram may be needed when creating the financial forecast model later, so any mistakes are corrected here.

For the profitability diagram shown below, we can see that profits were growing steadily even under the corona pandemic. I think this is a good sign when thinking about new businesses.

EXHIBIT 5: *Profitability Framework*

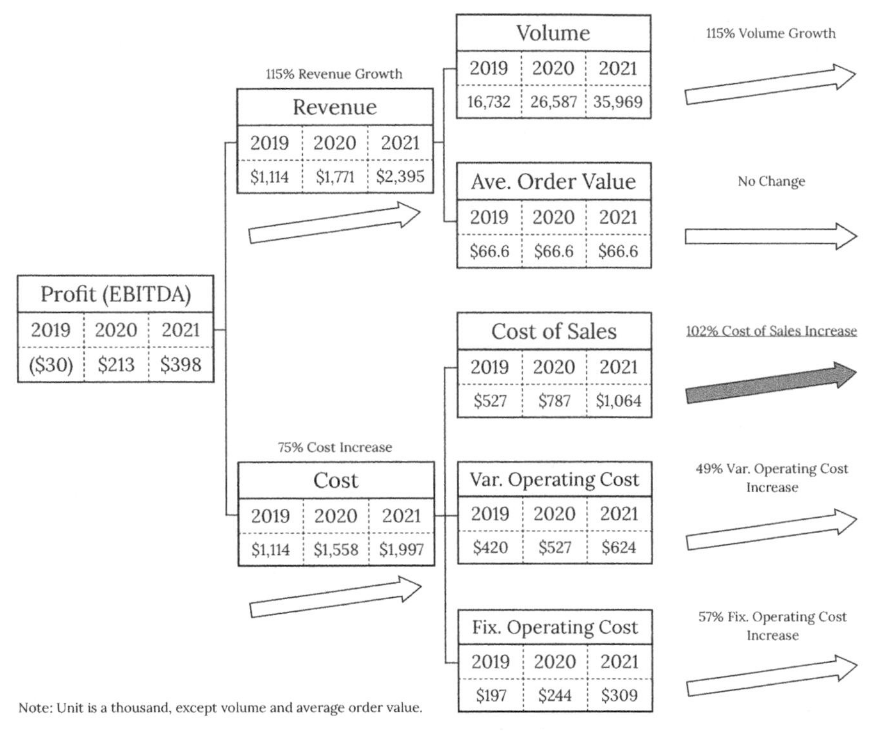

Note: Unit is a thousand, except volume and average order value.

However, what I was curious about was the high rate of increase in cost of sales. This may not be able to take full advantage of economies of scale, even though sales are increasing. Perhaps it was difficult to reduce the cost of goods sold because of the contract farmer's relationship. With that in mind, I think that the method of producing and selling agricultural products in-house was an advantage in terms of reducing variable costs and making the best use of economies of scale.

Since this data does not show cash flow, depreciation, capital structure, etc., I wanted to check the client's three financial statements later to create a robust financial model and perform a detailed analysis.

- New strawberry picking business
  - The diagram of the strawberry picking business model is as follows:

EXHIBIT 6: *Strawberry Picking Business Model*

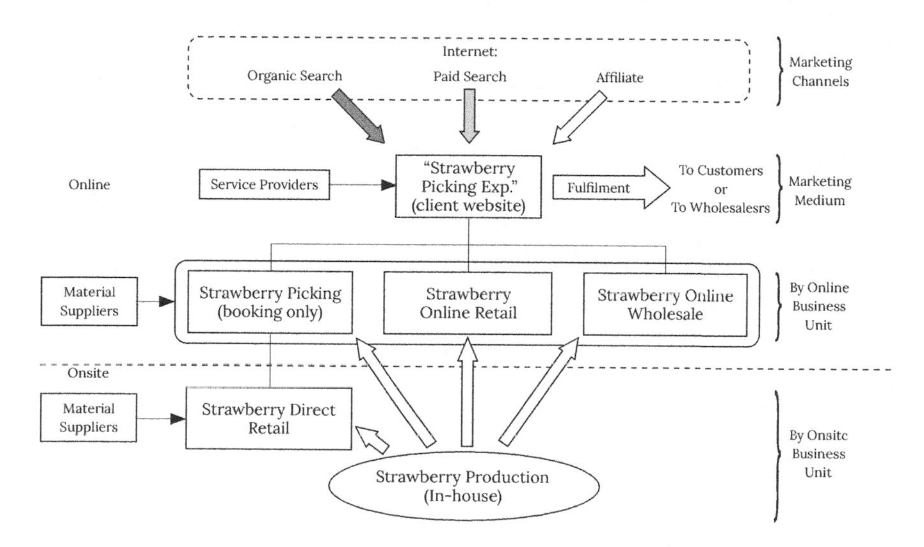

Similarly, if there were mistakes, I corrected them here.

- Preliminary estimation
  - Here are some of the estimated calculations I made:

EXHIBIT 7: *Estimation Excerpts*

E-COMMERCE ESTIMATION

Organic Search Monthly Estimates	**Assumptions**
Population of Washington state and surroundings	10,000,000
% who have internet access	70%
% who have credit card	90%
% who use search engine	90%

% who use google or bing service	95%
% who search & buy agri-products online	20%
% who search & buy lux agri-products online	50%
% who see client's HP link	20%
% who click on HP link	5%
Days in a month	30
Maximum monthly traffic estimates	**161,595**

STRAWBERRY PICKING ESTIMATION

Yearly Market Size Estimates	**Assumptions**
Population of Washington state and surroundings	10,000,000
% who are adults	50%
% who eat fruits	80%
% who eat luxury strawberry	15%
% who travel for strawberry picking	20%
# of orders per customer in year	1
# of ticket purchases per order	3
Price of strawberry picking	25
Maximum yearly market size estimates	**$9,000,000**

Yearly Revenue Estimates after 5 years	
Max strawberry picking market size estimation	9,000,000
% of client's market share in 5 years	10%
Yearly revenue estimates after 5 years	**$900,000**

INITIAL COST ESTIMATION

Initial Capital Expenditure Estimates	**Assumptions**
Initial capital expenditure unit price ($/ares)	12,000
Initial capital expenditure for 10 ares ($/10 ares)	120,000
Initial Capital expenditure for 1ha ($/1ha)	**$1,200,000**

Professional Fee Estimates	
Initial capital expenditure for 1ha ($/1ha)	1,200,000
Professional fee (% of initial capex)	15%
Professional fee (consultation, training, etc.)	**$180,000**

The main purpose of making estimates is to determine which drivers/levers (or variables) are impacting financial metrics such as revenue, costs, and thus, profit. For example, in e-commerce, site traffic is an important driver in sales forecasting.

Regarding the cost, I confirmed with the supplier that the estimated initial investment required for an area of 1 hectare is about $1.2 million. Considering the subsidy, the actual cost can be lower than this. This makes it easier for the client to imagine how much initial capital investment is needed.

It doesn't matter at all if the estimated figures don't match in reality, as I can fix them later. If we have a rough idea of how much, that's enough for now.

Recommendation

This completes Phase 0 work. At this stage, I have concluded that a new strawberry picking business should be considered further. All I have to do now is wait for a reply from the client and answer his questions, if any, and receive approval to proceed planning.

If the client's request and objective is clear here, it is possible to determine the key questions and issues, make hypotheses, find out what kind of data and graphs are needed for verification, and make a preliminary story. If the client is not sure about the decision-making criteria, the consultant may propose the criteria and support the decision.

I normally do a lot of analysis apart from the report. That is because there may be valuable information and insights there when I meet the client later. It's not a special one; it's a general analysis, like SWOT analysis, found in business books, so I'll omit it here.

With this much time and effort in the preparatory stage, the rest of the work will be much easier. Recall that at the beginning, I wrote that 50% of the work is in preparation.

PHASE 1: HISTORICAL AND FORECASTING E-COMMERCE BUSINESS

Now that the client has approved the continuation of the project, I moved on to the next phase.

The main purpose of Phase 1 is to share and verify existing data with clients. Most of the insights gained from the analytical work performed here would be familiar to the client, so I explained them concisely. Basically, what we do is improve the quality and quantity of the analysis performed in Phase 0.

I assumed that I had found a US consultant, called John, before Phase 1 began. Let's say he is also a member of FIRMSconsulting. It would be nice to have a common learning experience with those who work together as a team.

From here on, in addition to individual leadership, team leadership must be demonstrated. If John is a responsible and experienced consultant, we both respect each other, take leadership, and work together as equal team partners. If he is particularly good as a person and as a leader, I will gladly follow him. In that case, no special strategy or financial skills are required as I support him. If he is inexperienced, the priority is to satisfy our client's needs, so I would take the lead with top-down leadership. In this case, John is motivated and promising, but he's still young and has no farming experience, so I decided to work as a top-down leader.

[Subsequent work can be seen by clients hiring a strategy consultant, so I'll only summarize the work done and recommendations.]

Basically, what I did was receive the financial statements from the client, create a historical financial model, and conduct ratio analysis such as return on equity, commonly known as ROE. Return on equity consists of three drivers (or variables) that give an overall picture of the client's business: profitability, asset efficiency, and financial leverage (i.e., net income margin, total assets turnover ratio, and total assets to equity ratio respectively). In this case, we have found that the total assets turnover ratio and the total assets to equity ratio have decreased in the previous year.

Then, if possible, look at customer-related metrics in terms of customer acquisition costs, profit per order, lifetime value, and payback. We also examined the enterprise value (EV) of the client company using the discounted cash-flow (DCF) method. These analyses can be useful when conducting focus interviews with clients.

Creating a financial forecast model based on historical data is done in only one future scenario with the consent of the client. The reason is that clients are more familiar with their business and the industries they are involved in than strategy consultants.

At this stage, schedule focus interviews with the clients. Please note that the clients also evaluate the consultant through the interview. If they think we don't know anything, or that we don't think about the employees we work with, it can hinder our work later. The hypotheses and stories created in Phase 0 are also modified based on the client's information.

Finally, we make Phase 1 recommendations and confirm with the client whether to continue the consultation of this project. From the results of the forecast model analysis, we found that the profitability ratio and total asset turnover ratio are expected to decline in the future. Even if sales of the existing business continue to grow, economies of scale cannot be effectively utilized, and further profitability improvements are largely limited by external factors (e.g., fruit suppliers), so we as consultants have determined that it is well worth examining new businesses such as strawberry picking.

A dashboard that summarizes the analysis results is posted below. This is one of the deliverables to give to the client.

EXHIBIT 8: *E-Commerce Historical and Forecast Dashboard*

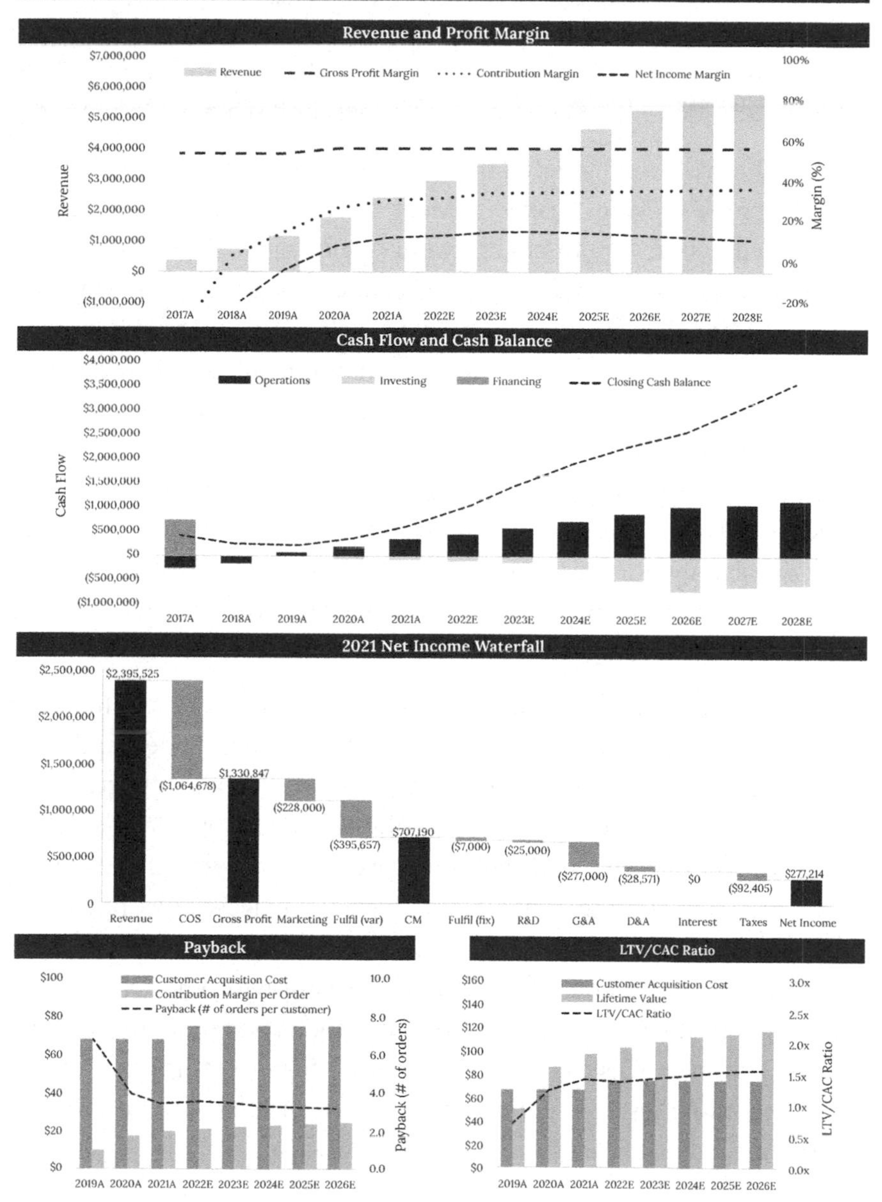

PHASE 2: FORECASTING NEW STRAWBERRY PICKING BUSINESS

After obtaining approval from the client, we considered the feasibility of a new strawberry picking business. Here, the secret to success is to work as a leader with a good grasp of ideals and reality.

Firstly, there is a fundamental thing to keep in mind when considering a strawberry picking business. Most business owners tend to be fascinated by the benefits of strawberry picking, high customer unit price, and low labor and packaging costs. It is a big attraction that there is no need to perform harvesting, selection, and packing work. However, it should be remembered that not all the strawberries produced can be used for strawberry picking. This is understandable when you think about what the customers are looking for. Customers want to eat as much as they like, surrounded by many strawberries. It is a tourism business, so our mission is to provide a fun experience that will satisfy our customers. Therefore, strawberries that cannot be used for strawberry picking must be sold by other means. Here we have considered retail and wholesale possibilities.

Secondly, in order to estimate sales and costs realistically, it is necessary to analyze from both sides of market demand and production supply, called "Top-Down Analysis" and "Bottom-Up Analysis" respectively. The reason why analysis from both sides is necessary is that demand-side analysis does not reveal the actual sales limit. On the other hand, supply-side analysis does not know how much market demand there is, so it is difficult to estimate how much sales trends should be. When working with clients who are familiar with the field, it is often better to focus on reality rather than ideals. However, this may not be the case for investors that bet on future possibilities. It depends on the needs of the customer, that is, where the value is placed.

The analysis method is not much different from Phase 1, so it will be omitted.

As a strategic consultant, I would recommend the strawberry picking business if the client can accept some of the concerns. For example, equity capital must first be set at $700,000 or more. Enterprise value of the strawberry picking business is one tenth that of e-commerce. Moreover, it takes more than ten years to recover initial capital expenditures.

We are assuming that 70% of the visitors to the newly created homepage are for strawberry picking, and the amount used for strawberry picking is 30% of the total production. We also assume that 50% of the initial agricultural capital investment is subsidized. If the client starts the business and deviates significantly from these conditions, such as no subsidy, the enterprise value is likely to be negative in the simulation.

By the way, if you do not think about the strawberry picking business at all and do business only by retailing or wholesale, the enterprise value can be significantly negative, which is obviously not good! The main reason is that the retail and wholesale unit prices are lower than the strawberry picking unit price, and the initial capital investment, especially the costs associated with environmental control systems, is too high. The website is designed to attract people who are interested in strawberry picking, so it is not optimized for retail or wholesale purposes. Furthermore, there is also harvesting, sorting, and packing work, which increases labor costs.

Before drawing any conclusions, we would like to integrate the two businesses, e-commerce and strawberry picking, in the next phase.

I don't feel the need to separate Phase 2 and the next Phase 3 meetings, so, I think they should be held concurrently, considering the convenience of the client.

EXHIBIT 9: *Strawberry Forecast Dashboard*

STRAWBERRY FORECAST DASHBOARD: CONSENSUS **EV: $353,832**

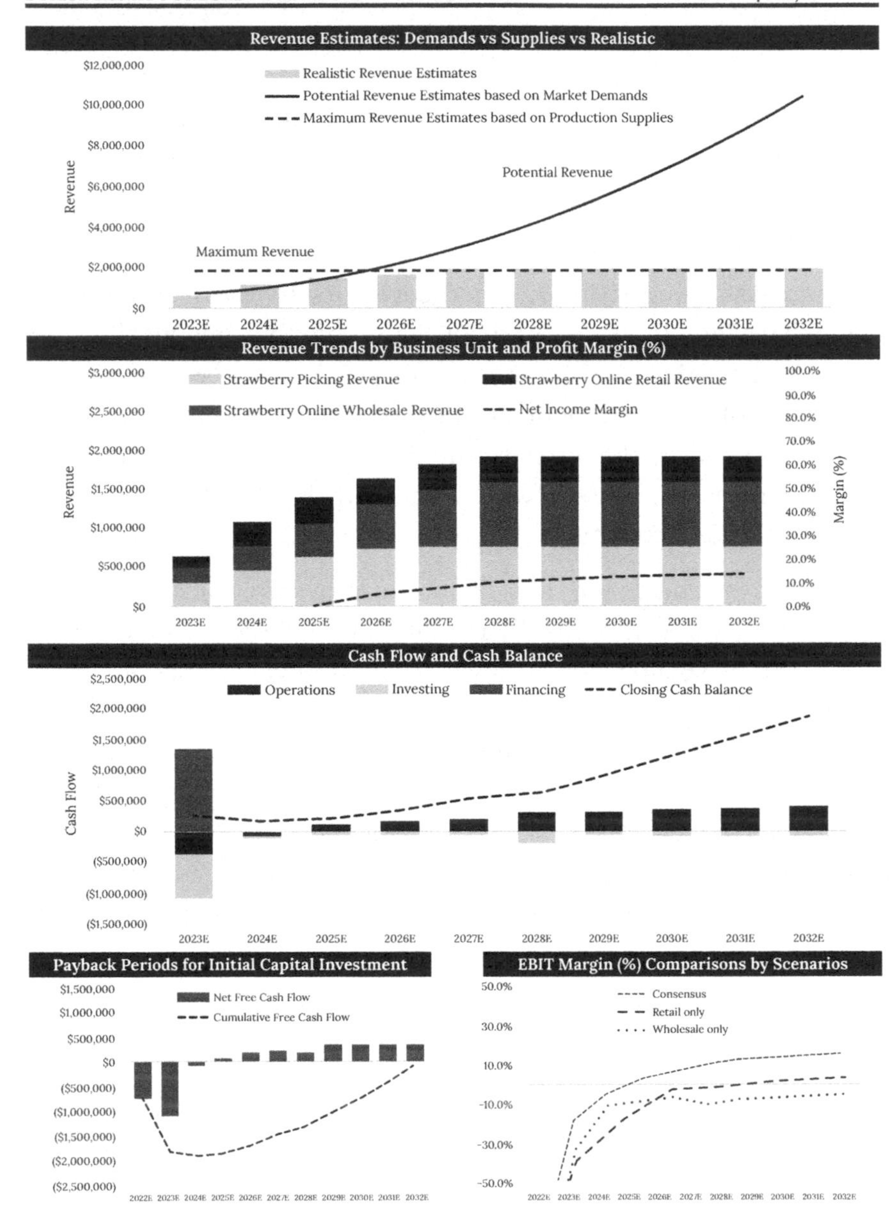

PHASE 3: CONSOLIDATING E-COMMERCE AND STRAWBERRY BUSINESS

At first, we created a financial forecast model that integrates the two businesses examined. There should be many valuable insights from the analyses so far. A few of them can be found by looking at the consolidated model dashboard below.

Most notable is the fact that the overall enterprise value does not change so much between the case where only the e-commerce business is continued as it is and the case where the strawberry picking business is carried out in addition. The reason is that the sales and profits of the strawberry picking business are generally smaller than those of the existing EC business in the first place. Furthermore, due to the large capital investment, depreciation costs are putting pressure on profits. Depending on the year, the profit margin may drop by nearly 10% of sales.

On the other hand, the people I met in agriculture weren't always working just to make money. Each person had different reasons, such as being fond of agriculture and nature, or having a philosophical belief. So, if the client has a strong desire for agriculture, we would like to offer some strategy and alternative options.

From a strategic point of view for finance, make a business plan on the assumption that subsidies will be issued preferably more than 50%, client's own equity funds of $700,000 or more, and funds are not generated through debt. For customers, don't spend too much on marketing. In particular, attracting customers through search advertising is a variable cost, making it difficult to make the most of economies of scale, so it is important to always check the cost-effectiveness. Regarding operations, strawberries are a crop that require a lot of manual work, but if you think positively, mechanization has not yet progressed and there is plenty of room for improvement. It is difficult for large companies to enter the market at present, so I think it is strategically effective to enter the market now and lay the foundation for competitive advantage in preparation for the practical application of machines in the future. And from the perspective of human resources, considering the scale of sales, I think that more than 10 people cannot be hired in an area of 1 hectare. Considering the production work, at least 7 people should be needed as agricultural workers. Ideally, everyone will be motivated and have farming experience.

We have found that the existing plan does not provide sufficient enterprise value, so we propose a few more alternative options:

A. Reducing the cost of environmental control systems by introducing DIY

B. Producing strawberries in the traditional way

C. Proceed with existing plans

D. Withdraw from the strawberry picking business project

For Option A, purchase a commercially available control board such as "Raspberry Pi" or "Arduino," connect sensors and relays, program it yourself, and build an environmental control/measurement system. Basic knowledge of IT such as programming (e.g., Python) and networking, electricity, and machinery is required. This reduces the initial capital investment albeit only slightly. If I was 10 years younger and had start-up funding, I would want to develop the system myself. In the future, I think AI, drone, and satellite sensing technologies will be further incorporated into environmental control systems. Such a project looks fun!

For Option B, if the client just wants to make a living from agriculture, I think the surest method is to grow strawberries in the old-fashioned way. I've heard this directly from a strawberry farmer before. I also feel the same when I look at the financial model created. However, I do not recommend it unless he is confident in his physical strength as hard physical labor will continue.

As a financial analyst, I wouldn't recommend the new strawberry picking business, as the analysis of the financial model shows. Even if the sales growth rate slows down and the profit margin declines in the future, I think it is better to continue with the existing e-commerce business, where products are mainly outsourced.

However, one thing to keep in mind as a strategist is that in the future there may be significant business opportunities when harvesting, sorting, and packing machines are put into practical use. There is also the idea of preparing presently and continuously to secure market share when that time comes. Moreover, we must not forget that freezing technology for transportation, such as when exporting, is improving year by year. Therefore, in the case of clients who have abundant capital and are making stable profits, it may be considered as one of the potential business options.

EXHIBIT 10: *Consolidated Historical and Forecast Dashboard*

CONSOLIDATED HISTORICAL & FORECAST DASHBOARD **EV: $4,348,550**

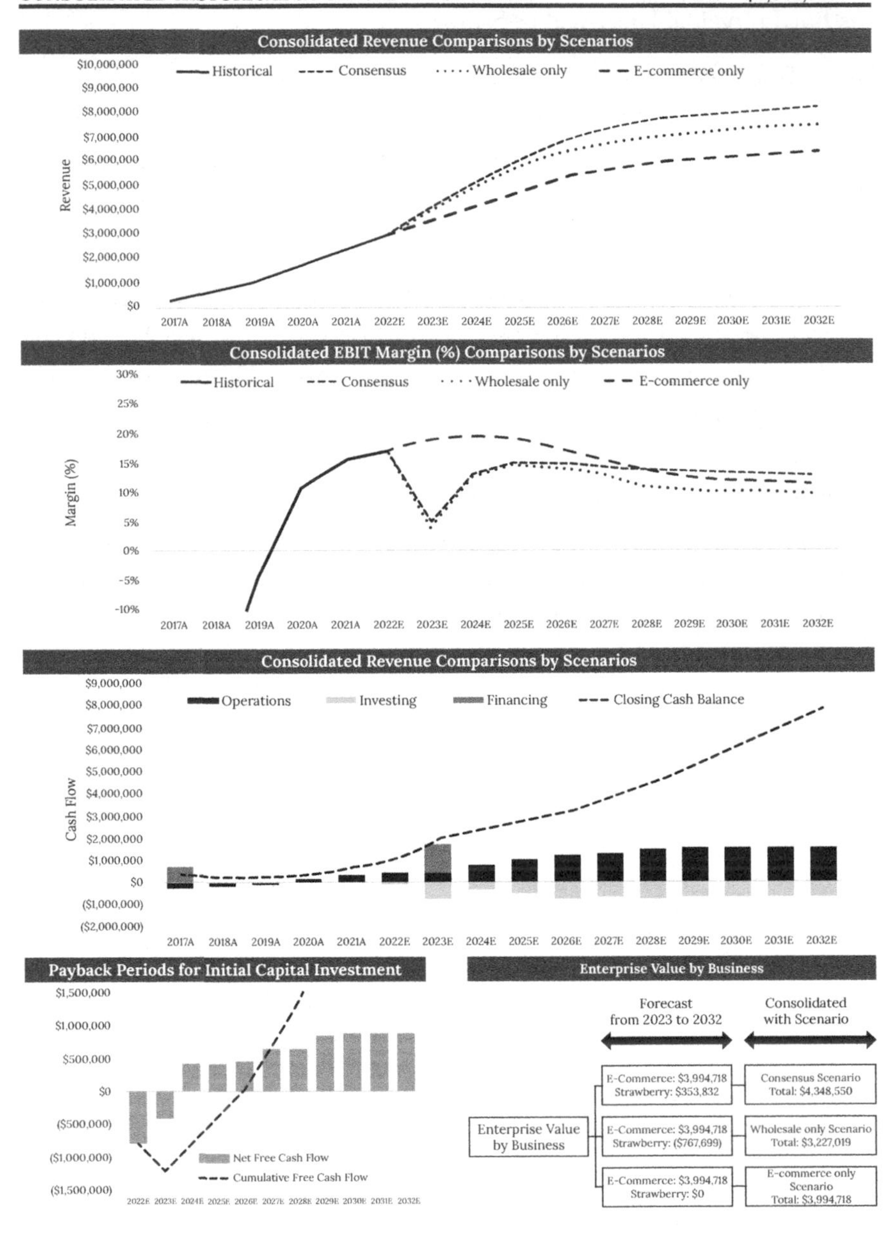

EXTRA PHASE: IMPLEMENTATION

If it is finally decided to start a strawberry picking business, we will move on to concrete planning. Of course, I think that the outline of what to do at this stage should be almost determined, but it may not be decided how to implement it yet.

Strategy consultants are generalists, so we are not very useful in the field. It's better to tell the client honestly this fact first. If I'm involved in on-site work, I'll do my best to support from behind. As you may have noticed, top-down leadership is not appropriate in this situation, so I need to show bottom-up leadership that respects the thinking in the field.

CONCLUSION

That concludes my chapter. I have packed in as much experience as possible. I apologize I couldn't write in detail due to the limited number of pages. This is what I wanted to read when I was younger.

The purpose of this chapter was twofold; one was to show how important theory is in practice as a leader, and the second was to give an overview of my business strategy and financial analysis based on those theories. If I could have discovered the big picture earlier in my career, I might have been able to work more effectively and not make many mistakes.

As a leader, it is important to know what type you are, as the Greek temple of Apollo also says, "Know thyself." I think that knowing oneself is one of our goals and may be the truth of mankind that transcends time.

It's very important to find someone you can truly respect. It helps your heart when you are in trouble. Professional consultants need to listen carefully to their clients and hand over accurate, high-quality deliverables. For that purpose, skills and know-hows are important, but before that, we must fully recognize that it is a job that supports the business of others. Basically, I think that people who like helping people are better suited to the profession of consultant.

In general, leaders need to have both good intuition and logic. Intuition is not easily acquired by some people because it is influenced by their natural qualities, but logical thinking can be improved by effort. Don't underestimate financial skills because you're a leader. In reality, many clients are looking for people who can read numbers and analyze scientifically.

Business skills, including leadership, can be learned from a variety of experiences. For example, I originally majored in electrical and computer engineering at university. And the project I was involved in was designing a telemetry subsystem for a microsatellite and was the leader of that team. So, most of my knowledge about business was self-taught.

Did you notice that the case studies presented in this chapter were based on my leadership theory? Financial statements and financial models have been newly created for this. Therefore, the figures such as sales and profits are fictitious for demonstration, but mathematically, they are connected properly. Please be cautious when using it as a reference for your own business as it differs from the actual results; use your own data in practice.

Here, I focused on individual leadership rather than the commonly imagined team leadership. It is because individual leadership is a prerequisite for team leadership. A good leader should be able to work alone, not just as a team.

The charts and graphs posted on the dashboards have their own reasons, so I wanted to explain them one by one. Also, I wanted to dig a little deeper into the workflow with John, a consultant in the US, in terms of leadership.

Estimation and hypothetical thinking are powerful tools for leaders who need to solve real problems timely and communicate to gain understanding and consent. This is a skill that can be acquired depending on the training, so I recommend it to everyone regardless of occupation. The publisher, FIRMSconsulting, is also an education resource, so if you are interested, please consider registering as a member. If you would like to know more about creating financial models and building business strategies, it is my specialty, so you can contact me, and I will be happy to assist you.

The case studies presented here are usually jobs that I spend months on, taking into account interactions with clients and stakeholders. If you are new to strategy and financial analysis, you may find it difficult, but I think it is very useful knowledge for a lot of people, so don't be afraid to try it.

Although not covered in this chapter, I feel that many of the issues that businesspeople actually have are caused by human emotions. If they are solved, I often think that we can expect a drastic improvement in management performance, but it is a qualitative problem and not a quantitative problem that can be solved by an external consultant. So, I didn't go into too much about it here.

Of course, just as everyone has weaknesses, so do I. In my case, I'm basically not good at standing out, so sales and marketing are my weaknesses. It has been so since I was a kid. It is very important to be honest to provide the right value to our customers.

I wrote this information for people who are ordinary like me, but who are willing to learn and work hard. Here is some advice that my grandmother used to say when I was a kid:

"Read a lot of books. You can't compete with someone who reads a lot of books."

I hope you have learned something.

Thank you very much for reading.

AUTHOR BIO

Takahiro Ajimizu is a global financial strategist in Japan, specializing in business strategy, financial analysis, and IT with many years of international experience.

In 2021, he launched the "Zen Consulting" internet service, which integrates his various experiences and provides high-quality financial strategies that help our customers succeed in their businesses.

He designed and developed a corporate website as a leader in his e-commerce project. It has grown into a site visited by over 15,000 unique users per month within a few years.

In the agricultural project, Takahiro cultivated Chinese herbs, translated technical materials for cutting-edge environmental control systems imported from overseas, and offered operational support for those systems.

He not only developed new products and created marketing plans for existing products, but also designed guidelines with reference to HACCP (Hazard Analysis and Critical Control Point) for food safety.

In government and local government subsidies, Takahiro compiled the materials and all applications have been accepted so far.

He graduated from Queensland University of Technology in Australia with a major in electrical and computer engineering. He participated in a microsatellite development project, commonly known as JAESat, as a leader in the telemetry subsystem.

Connect With Takahiro: How was the content of my chapter?

I'm now curious about how you felt after reading this. So, I've decided that if you send your impressions or feedback, I will send you the three financial statements (i.e., income statement, balance sheet, and cash flow statement) prepared for this document as a bonus. Some people may want to check the content themselves using those statements for study or business.

Please contact me at info@zen-consulting.net by March 31, 2023.

In addition, I have found new business improvements from this content, and I will incorporate them into my consulting and financial services. If you find my chapter interesting, please also visit the website (https://zen-consulting.net/).

CHAPTER 8

Clarity, Displine and Consistency

BY DUDDY ABDULLAH

IN THIS CHAPTER, I would like to share a few lessons that I've used to build my career and establish myself as a leader. Through synthesizing my knowledge and experiences, I've distilled the majority of my learning into three simple principles that guide all of my actions. I hope that you can use them just as I have, and that they can help support you on your own journey to success.

The first lesson is to begin with the end in mind. What legacy do you want to leave? What impact do you want your actions to have on your family, the community, and the world? Why does it matter? These questions are important for building long-term navigation tools that will help you dispel roadblocks and establish inner clarity.

Secondly, be respectful. Sincerity and empathy are crucial tools in even the most challenging environments. This concept deals with overarching values that will not only propel your career faster, but also allow you to empower yourself by way of empowering others.

Lastly, identify your operating model. Be mindful of limiting beliefs, maintain focus by way of reducing distractions, and create optionality by reducing leverage exuded upon you by external influences. Here, I'll address ideas of consistency as it applies to short-term daily habit creation, and the rejection of implicit biases.

In short, these three lessons concern the clarity in 'why,' the discipline in 'how,' and the consistency in 'what.'

BEGINNING AT THE END

There are certain things that everybody wants in their lives. A fulfilling career, healthy family relationships, financial freedom, education for our children, a valuable social network... the list goes on. Since it's impossible to know the directions that your life will take, the prospect of achieving so much can be a staggering one. We have no way of knowing what lies ahead, but can we still dare to contemplate the legacy that we might leave behind for our families, our community, and our world? Maybe the process of strategizing our life in order to reach our fullest potential should actually start on the other end of everything. In other words, how can we learn to live by preparing to die?

When I break down the idea of a legacy, I find that there are three main questions to be addressed:

- How can I tap into a pool of 'divine' wisdom in order to fight inertia and recharge my motivation when it becomes depleted?

- How can I create family values and culture that will support my legacy?
- How does living with integrity allow me to maintain positive momentum and continual development of my skills?

Let's look at each of these questions in a little more depth.

WISDOM VERSUS INERTIA

When I think about the potential use of 'divine' wisdom to combat inertia and inspire motivation, I like to use a framework introduced in Simon Sinek's book *Start With Why*. Sinek eloquently argues that truly successful businesses have three key traits: clarity in WHY, discipline in HOW, and consistency in WHAT.

Our WHY, at its core, is what motivates us. In order to go about identifying it, we need to look at something greater than ourselves.

When I was growing up, my favorite books were a comic collection from a local publisher in Indonesia. They detailed the lives of important figures in history, including Isaac Newton, Mahatma Gandhi, Nelson Mandela, Wolfgang Amadeus Mozart, and the Wright Brothers. Every one of these people had a distinct WHY that led them to great achievements—achievements that would be remembered and celebrated for centuries to come. What were their methods of finding a truly revolutionary WHY that transcended time and cemented them as key players in the history of humankind?

One important thing to know is that your WHY cannot come from a place of fear. Fear is a paralyzing driver that will compel us to avoid things, thereby missing out on life's greatest opportunities. We need to fight against it by thinking proactively about the reason that we want to have an impact in the world. Remember that nobody can judge your WHY. It's for your purposes alone. The more honest you are in finding your WHY, the less impact other people's opinions will have on your motivation.

As important as it is to clarify your WHY, it's only the first step in the process of achieving success in your life. The way to do this is through building your HOW and your WHAT. Without a strong sense of HOW and WHAT, you'll find that you struggle to execute your ideas, no matter how brilliant they may be.

To understand these concepts, consider the analogy of achieving consensus in a boardroom meeting. The HOW is the corporate strategy by which the CEO and other executives translate the boardroom's mandate into actions: entering an optimal market, allocating resources to maximize a company's comparative advantage, minimizing risk, and creating KPIs in each business unit. The WHAT is the business unit strategy, which is concerned with the consistency of output through certain measures of quality, including operational and financial goals. Companies can make faster decisions when they have a solid alignment between clarity of shareholders' mandates, focused corporate strategy, and consistency of output produced by business unit strategy. These companies have a filtering system built into their framework, so that anything that doesn't correspond with their WHY, HOW, and WHAT will be rejected. Considering this, it becomes apparent that governance, while it may seem to be a solely administrative matter, is truly all about strategy.

It should come as no surprise that greater team engagement is the result of a strong company culture. When everyone works toward the same goal and trusts other team members, the road to success is a clear one. *Trust* is the key word here. Strong culture is less about having the right or wrong people on the bus, and more about creating an environment that allows individuals in the organization to go above and beyond by trusting each other. When people genuinely believe in organizational values, they're much more effective at sustaining a cultural legacy.

On the flip side, it's very dangerous to manipulate values and culture. When individuals feel cheated by the system, they could go to such measures as destroying shareholders' value. Even worse, the organization will have a troubled leadership transition. This is fatal to a company's chances of success because the new leader will be unlikely to continue the value system—which makes sense, seeing as a betrayal of that value system is what brought them to the role in the first place.

Starting from WHY can be hard, since it involves a lot of introspection, inspiration, vision, and clarity. Honesty fosters authenticity, authenticity fosters trust, trust fosters innovation, innovation fosters value, and value fosters legacy. If your organization does not have an honest WHY, it will struggle to create a sustainable culture of innovation. As a result, it will become a commodity of producing the WHAT, leaving it prone to disruption.

FAMILY VALUES

When talking about legacy, we can't remove family from the equation. Family is a formal and social unit that will be drastically impacted by your presence or the absence thereof. However, when we're building careers or endeavoring to change the world, our family life tends to become compartmentalized. This is always a mistake. The biggest and most valuable investment that you can make is with your family and significant others, as they will be the ones continuing your legacy.

Achievement-driven professionals often fall into the trap of believing that they can minimize investment in their personal lives in order to give more attention to the success of their careers. However, professionals who skip out on participating in their children's intellectual development will miss a critical opportunity to provide those children with a step up once they're starting school. Kids pick up on values and information when they're ready to learn; the problem is that we can't predict when that will be. The best thing to do is to be with your children as much as possible so that you don't waste your chance when it comes.

One of the most powerful ways to build family values is by respecting the sacrifices made by the generations before us. Our parents and elders worked hard throughout their lives to ensure that their families would continue to thrive once their own time was done. Laying a strong generational foundation is what enables a family to act as a cohesive unit, in which every member is important, and everyone respects one another's endeavors. While no family member is perfect, all are deserving of respect. The sacrifices that we make for each other's happiness and success serve as the glue that holds the family together.

My extended family often tells me stories about my mother's career as a banking system analyst. In the 1980s, she was so successful that she received scarcity skills benefits. When my twin and I were born, a balance between her career and her family became incredibly hard to maintain; she once told me that the hardest feeling is listening to your children cry when she needed to leave for work. Later in my life, once I was college-aged, my father had to switch jobs in order to be able to send me and my brother to study in Australia. My parents had a strict rule that my siblings and I were not allowed to work while in school, since it would distract us from our learning. Instead, they worked harder than ever in order to provide for us.

Building culture in a family is the same as building it in an organization: We need to have a focus on the reward mechanism. Children are our program in a sense. If we condition them to feel as though they're entitled to something, they'll lack gratitude; if we teach them to show off, we instill them with false confidence and inhibit their ability to empathize. Gratitude, empathy, and humility are crucial ingredients when it comes to finding inspiration for our WHY, which in turn serves as the key to building a powerful career and a lasting legacy.

LIVING WITH INTEGRITY

There's no disputing the fact that, in order to build a powerful career, we'll need to solve complex and difficult problems. Building these skills isn't easy, and the opportunity to learn them is a luxury and privilege in and of itself. While constructing our career, many of us will face insecurities from our peers, global competition pools, market conditions, and—most importantly—self-doubts. When our self-doubts control us, it will impact our career performance, and we may find ourselves tempted to take shortcuts that have negative repercussions in the long run.

There are two questions to be answered when dealing with this struggle. Firstly, how do we ensure that we're staying on the right track and avoiding ethical mishaps? And secondly, what must we do in order to continuously develop within that path?

Clayton Christensen suggests that the key to making ethical decisions and staying on the right track is to recognize and avoid marginal thinking whenever possible in your personal and professional life. "Marginal thinking" is defined as a type of thinking that tends to focus on short-term benefits or costs but fails to consider the full consequences of actions taken. This manifests in the act of making small, seemingly harmless decisions or compromises, which then tend to lead to bigger, often catastrophic results, from business failures to jail time. This type of thinking can be classified into two main realms:

opting against marginal profit and opting for marginal cost. Both of these can have devastating effects, even if they seem negligible at the time. Maintaining personal integrity and minimizing marginal thinking is what enables us to create a conducive environment in which to build our skills, therefore making the process of acquiring those skills no more difficult than it needs to be.

The second question concerns building momentum within our skill sets and making continual progress. The underlying principle here is that success is built over time by way of executing small disciplines on a consistent basis. Keep in mind that the contrary is also true: When you neglect simple disciplines, you will also inhibit growth. In other words, it's a matter of building habits. However, doing so is a lot harder than it may seem.

There's a lot of science behind the formation of habits. While it may be worthwhile to do some of your own research in that area, I personally make use of one simple tip to ensure that I'm developing and improving myself on a daily basis. Every day, I identify one important thing that I accomplished. Sometimes, life will throw us so many surprises that we feel as if we're spiraling out of control. We can battle this with consistency, by journaling one achievement or new skill every day. We can then also be inspired by looking back on our writing and seeing how far we've come.

If someone had given me this piece of advice when I was first starting my career, I believe that I could have accomplished even more at this point in my life. It's my sincere hope that you'll be able to make use of this lesson in order to lead a more content, meaningful, and powerful life.

BEING RESPECTFUL

Shortly after completing my undergraduate degrees, I joined a program that aimed to give back to the community by teaching elementary school in a remote Indonesian village for one year. This program aimed to address a problem with the distribution of teachers that was prominent at the time. When it was launched, 66% of elementary schools in the more remote areas of Indonesia were suffering from a lack of teachers. Through aiding this problem, it was our goal to instill the hope of a better future for the children. The underlying philosophy of the program was that the issue of education is not only the responsibility of the government, but of every educated citizen.

What I certainly didn't expect was to be posted in a region that had a history of military conflict. I may have just been teaching elementary school but doing so in a place that served as a base for military insurgency was no elementary matter at all, particularly considering the social wounds that remained prominent in the village. The challenges that I faced throughout this experience taught me valuable lessons concerning empathy, respect, and leadership, which I've distilled into the following three points:

- Being powerless always feels bad, but it's a very powerful tool when it comes to building empathy.
- Tri-sector stakeholder engagement is complex. To navigate it, you need to be sincere, find a role model, and create a local champion in order to build sustainable impact.
- Different people have different philosophies regarding tradition and ways of life. When entering new territory, you must always aim to be as respectful as possible.

BEING POWERLESS

One afternoon, after I had finished my teaching for the day, I was alarmed to see that several concerned-looking people were gathered around my host family's home. I soon learned that the daughter of my host parents was undergoing a medical emergency: She had been suffering from severe breathing problems, which were severe enough that she'd fainted three times. There were no proper hospitals in our vicinity. The only option was to put her on a mattress on top of a pick-up truck, and then drive her for hours along the red soil roads, which were slippery and precarious from the previous night's rain.

The helplessness that I felt in that moment was heightened by a memory of my time studying in Australia. One day, I'd been getting out of a tram on my way to campus when I heard a loud noise coming from overhead. It was a helicopter, transporting a patient to the Royal Melbourne Hospital as swiftly and safely as possible. There was no fair comparison to be made between the infrastructure of Australia and Indonesia, and yet I found myself wishing that I could somehow provide similar aid for this person, whom I'd come to view as a family member.

The best I could do, however, was accompany my host family on the drive to the hospital. I sat in the front passenger seat, with my host father driving, while my host mother sat beside her daughter, crying from fear. As we drove, my host father said something to me that I've never forgotten: "Now you understand why we had the conflict; there isn't even a proper road built for our village!"

My host father was not an easy person to get along with. In the first month that I stayed with him and his family, I ended up being hospitalized on multiple occasions due to my body's struggles with adapting to food and other living conditions. His response was to sarcastically ask me whether I was growing fond of the bed in the hospital, suggesting that perhaps it was better than the one he had provided for me. But I never took his comments personally because I knew that they were a result of how powerless he felt. Eventually, we forged a very close bond, and we both cried when I was forced to leave due to an escalated security risk preceding a local election.

Experiencing moments of helplessness can build empathy, since you can spot when others may be experiencing the same things that you've been through. When you effectively leverage your ability to empathize, you'll discover a powerful source of inspiration for your WHY. This can be easily translated into the business world: By being able to identify pain points in the communities of both your customers and your employees, you can improve the services, products, and methods of your organization.

STAKEHOLDER ENGAGEMENT

Most of the people that I came to know during my time in the village were very poor. They could only afford to eat meat three times a year, during important religious celebrations. On the Day of Arafah, one of the rare times when fathers would purchase meat for their families, I was summoned to the city for an urgent matter. I was having trouble finding transportation until it was offered to me by an older villager.

Pak Idris was an honorary teacher. This was a title given to a teacher without formal civil servant status, who only received an inconsistent honorary fee for their work. On that day, instead of seeking out labor to procure the additional income necessary to buy meat, he gave me a ride to the city and back on his motorcycle. It was an old machine that overheated every 30 minutes or so, but it got the job done. Once we made it back to the village, I served him water and asked him to accept a stipend. He refused me adamantly.

"When I drove you around, it was because I wanted to help you," he said. "Now, I would like to find ways to make some money to buy meat." At this point, it was already afternoon, but he was still determined to find any work that he could. I would later insist that he accepted my stipend, but his words from that day still stuck with me.

Pak Idris was a very simple elder, but a very special one as well. He was welcomed by all members of the village, as well as those belonging to neighboring communities. His sincerity and ingenuity earned him the trust of everyone he met. Due to the issue of his constantly overheating motorcycle, he often had to make pit stops during his travels, giving him opportunities to foster relationships with the occupants of several different villages. This was a society deeply wounded by its history of civil and military conflict, and trust was a scarce commodity; suspicions still ran high that one family would report another to authorities. Yet this one man seemed to navigate seamlessly between opposing factions.

Despite being one of the poorer people in the village, he had the advantage of seeing people for their true selves. He could go to places relatively unnoticed, without triggering defense mechanisms from others. He helped me to understand that people without any real money, education, or bragging rights are the most honest of all because they don't think that they need to impress us. In turn, they tend to recognize us for what we really are.

Pak Idris's story can help us learn a foundational building block to help navigate our interactions with stakeholders: sincerity. Of course, empathy and sincerity alone are not enough to create impactful initiatives. Engaging in such initiatives is complex, and executives are advised to find role models who have successfully navigated seamless tri-sector transitions. Building instinctive judgment takes a lot of time, and every local context presents its own challenges. By finding successful role models, especially ones who can offer personal mentorship, leaders can significantly reduce their learning curve and avoid costly mishaps.

Having navigated the complexity of the stakeholders' engagement and determined the strategic course of action to be taken, the next step is to create sustainable impact. In order to do this, we need to provide the opportunity for local champions to emerge and manage the initiatives. The same goes for organizations within our careers. We must always work to prepare for the delegation and ultimately the transition of leadership. The continual impact of an organization's legacy relies on the success of such transitions.

TRADITIONAL HOUSE PHILOSOPHY

A final insight that I would like to share regarding my experience in that village concerns the philosophy of its traditional house. When I arrived, many presumptions were made about my purpose and intentions. Some people thought that I was an army intelligence officer sent from Jakarta, while others suspected me of being a preacher of false teachings, come to spread lies to the village. When I entered the community, the first lesson I learned was to apply the philosophy of the traditional wooden house.

This type of house has a very specific method of construction, with particular expectations regarding how to approach it. A steep wooden staircase leads up to the front door. Before entering, one is expected to knock three times and send their greetings to the residents. Once they answer and welcome you, you're free to enter. Since the door typically isn't very tall, you need to lower your head to step inside, assuming a posture similar to a slight bow. All of these traditions are representative of the emphasis that the society puts on the respect of a house's owner and on their role in providing warmth and protection under which their family can safely grow.

Once I had come to understand unique social traditions such as this one, I asked the local religious leader to let me join his teachings every day. This also served as an effective strategy to win the trust of the community. In doing so, I was finally able to overcome the misconceptions placed upon me by the villagers, all while learning about the delicate social reality of a post-conflict society.

While traditions and cultures are infinitely varied, some values are universal. Sincerity, empathy, and respect are the languages that transcend beyond all borders, whether they be cultural, linguistic, geographical, or sociological.

DEFINING AN OPERATING MODEL

When reflecting upon our careers and our experience with leadership, we'll sometimes feel disheartened or overwhelmed. We may find that the place where we now stand is nowhere near that toward which we initially aspired. It's not unusual to feel as though we've wasted time or to ponder upon the lost potential of every missed opportunity. When I look back on my personal journey, I can identify three powerful lessons:

- Focusing our effort on input accountability will reduce the leverage of our self-doubt.
- The sooner we can define our operating models, the better; things outside of our core decision-making criteria should be

treated as a distraction, and therefore must be rejected.

- We must create optionality by minimizing others' potential to derail us from our critical path. Instead, we need to identify our skills and find how we can best use them to our advantage.

FOCUSING ON INPUT ACCOUNTABILITY

One of the biggest obstacles standing between us and our notion of success is self-doubt. We all have ingrained perceptions of reality that we believe to be true, even when that isn't necessarily the case. These can impede us from reaching our potential by imposing imaginary constraints. The longer we hesitate to act on our potential, the higher the compounded opportunity costs become, preventing us from achieving more and more important milestones.

When living in a capitalist society, there's one question that we need to ask ourselves: Am I a consumer or a merchant? Whenever you procrastinate the act of venturing forth to build sustainable skills for yourself, the longer you tend to be stuck in the role of the consumer. Of course, all of us are consumers to some extent, considering the roles that we take in the value chain. But do we become a terminal consumer, or can we find ways to turn the resources that we consume into potentially valuable input that could be monetized to someone, somewhere?

I find that the consideration of this question serves as a powerful paradigm shift, due to the way that its binary approach forces us to be brutally honest in the evaluation of our implicit beliefs. The most common of these beliefs is a feeling of unpreparedness, like we aren't ready to accomplish something yet. The result of this is that we tend to be stuck in the learning zone, thus limiting entrepreneurial spirit and initiatives. In the context of capitalism, those who take calculated risks will be rewarded. Be aware of the impediments that we subconsciously create on our path toward leadership and fulfillment; many of them are tricks of our own minds.

The subliminal tendency to delay taking initiative comes from the avoidance of failure, but it also denies us the sweetness of success. We fear being ridiculed by naysayers, but the truth is that they're more concerned with their own failures than they are with ours. While the output of our efforts is determined by many factors beyond our control, we alone are responsible for our input. The challenge lies in staying disciplined and honest enough to take accountability for that input and its consequences.

Take massive, messy actions. Learn from mistakes. Make adjustments so that you can do better next time. Waiting for "the perfect moment" to do something is an illusion that entraps us in inertia. Oftentimes, the problem with procrastination is figuring out how to get started with a task in the first place. If you find yourself in this situation, try utilizing a five-minute productivity hack, in which you set aside five minutes to put the entirety of your focus on starting a task. Once you've broken that initial barrier, the rest of it is likely to come much more easily.

Unfortunately, no economic model includes a workaround for overcoming limited resources. In fact, the study of economics itself examines how individuals, societies, and governments can maximize their utility functions under the pressure of constrained resources. There are finite opportunities available to us, and market participants must work to anticipate and prepare themselves to exploit opportunities when they do arise. The key is to keep your development wheel in motion, so that you're always ready to seize your chance when it does come along.

With limiting beliefs taken out of the equation, we may still struggle under the weight of unmet aspirations. My response to this is that we should remind ourselves that we're in control of how we spend our own time. If we calm ourselves and focus on adhering to an input system, we will make progress. This warrants a comparison to professional athletes' differentiation between goals and system. An athlete's goals may be manifested in the form of a gold medal, but they need to focus on the system of their training regimen in order to accomplish them. We may want to do several things at once or take unrealistically large steps to improve our skill set, but that often isn't possible, especially considering the constraints put upon us from other areas in our lives. Instead, build tactile steps. For example, you might set yourself up with a system in which you spend two hours every weeknight studying programming for the next three months. So long as you can consistently provide that input, your skills are guaranteed to develop, no matter how slow the process may feel. To quote a favorite saying from my parents: "There is a blessing in consistency."

At one point in my career, my employer told me that I could quickly become rich by being a broker of capital, land, contracts, and so on. However, unless your endeavors are institutionalized, your wealth cannot be sustainable—and institutionalizing commercial ventures is never a short-term endeavor. There's no easy workaround or cheat code to success, and if you seem to have found one, it's worthwhile to take a moment and ask yourself whether or not that success is sustainable.

Short-termism tends to mislead us into thinking that what we seek lies entirely in the output or destination of a process. The way to create a truly sustainable system of personal development, however, is to find happiness in the process itself. In other words, our focus should be on the journey more so than the destination.

When we feel unsettled or unfulfilled, we need to acknowledge it as a good sign. It reflects the strength of our aspirations and signals that we know how full potential is much greater than our current life might reflect. In order to build sustainable improvement, we need to create a system that focuses on taking accountability for input goals, having a long-term mindset, and, most importantly, enjoying ourselves along the way.

DEFINING OPERATING MODELS

In recent times, humanity has gotten faster at adapting due to increased literacy and widespread access to information flow; the world's ability to change outpaces our ability to adapt to those changes. As a result of this, we need an operating model that acts as a filtering mechanism, allowing us to create valuable optionality without being distracted by pursuing different opportunities. Distraction, after all, wastes the most precious commodity of them all: time.

My own personal operating model consists of 10 value systems. In order for me to deem an opportunity worthy of pursuit, it must meet all of the criteria described below. I advise you to work with your significant others in order to create a coherent value system that functions both personally and professionally.

1. Family comes first.
    - Sustain safety and mutual respect.
    - Sustain personal developments.
    - Sustain comfort and happiness.
2. Be honest.
    - Your word is your bond; do not break your contracts or the law.

- Pay your taxes on time; minimize, and don't evade.
- Being honest 100% of the time is infinitely better than being honest 98% of the time.

3. Be humble and kind.
    - Don't be a jerk.
    - Respect greater forces. Many of the world's most influential leaders exist under the radar, and karma tends to find its way back to you.
    - Utilize empathy as a comparative advantage. It will help you identify pain points and nonverbal cues.
4. Trust your inner voice when evaluating others.
    - Good people tend to lead to positive environments.
    - Positive environments lead to positive developments.
    - Positive developments lead to meaningful impacts.
5. Execute things well.
    - Guard your name and reputation.
    - Choose minimization of risk over maximization of gain.
    - Maintain your momentum; consistency of one success leads to another.
6. Build a superstar team instead of operating as an individual.
    - Avoid loss aversion bias: Avoid being in a huge sunk cost situation.
    - Avoid overconfidence bias: Seek input from your loved ones, who tend to have the best intentions.
    - Avoid conformity bias: Promote dissenting opinions to

neutralize anyone's personal bias.

7. Stay focused on productivity.
    - Eliminate tasks.
    - Automate tasks.
    - Delegate tasks.
8. Sleep well.
    - We cannot cheat death.
    - Therefore, we cannot cheat health.
    - Therefore, we cannot cheat sleep.
9. Live sustainably for the long-term.
    - Keep your cash flow positive. Avoid debts, except mortgage, but settle early.
    - Don't live on the edge; maintain a minimum of a one-year emergency fund.
    - Respect nature and think of the environmental legacy being left for your children.
10. Be grateful.
    - Acknowledge the importance of being able to eat, work, and sleep under a roof.
    - Appreciate the fact that we have internet access and globally accepted credit cards.
    - Value the time that we have to spend with our families.

CREATING OPTIONALITY BY REDUCING LEVERAGE

At this point, we've identified strategies for breaking free of our limiting beliefs. We've also examined the ways that operating models can be used to eliminate distractions. The final important point concerns the leverage exerted upon us by other people.

First of all, how should we define leverage? The academics of finance teach us that there are two main classifications: operational and financial. Operational leverage can be further broken down into two categories: direct and indirect.

Living sustainably is the best solution for avoiding the impact of leverage, particularly household's direct operational leverage. I personally define sustainability as the ability to consistently provide for my family members without damaging anyone's interests, including those of the natural world. A livable level of comfort may be subjective, but everyone who takes part in sustaining a family is faced with the question of how much we can sustainably contribute to the provision of that comfort. Living sustainably has close associations with long-term thinking and self-restraint, both of which grow easier with practice. Contingency plans are also valuable when it comes to avoiding this sort of leverage. Once safety is no longer a concern, it becomes much easier to deal with personal developments and the creation of wealth.

A more subtle but extremely important lesson involves indirect operational leverage. I define indirect operational leverage as sets of personal biases that hamper an individual's decision-making performance. One day in Fontainebleau, I attended a class on behavioral finance that left me with several valuable takeaways. It began with an extensive review of the personal biases that affect our decision-making process. Three stood out to me in particular. The first, loss aversion bias, refers to our tendency to associate the pain of losing to be twice as powerful as the pleasure of gaining. The second, overconfidence bias, is the issue of overstating our ability, especially in situations where we need to make critical decisions. The third, conformity bias, is defined as our desire to seek comfort in a group of like-minded thinkers, which avoids the discomfort of dissent at the cost of creating a social or professional echo chamber. Teams are more than the sum of their parts, but only if they're constructed of individuals with differing strengths, beliefs, and abilities.

We previously discussed limiting beliefs, which may seem similar to leverage. I differentiate them in the following way: Limiting beliefs puts us in a state of inertia, rendering us unable to so much as start down a path to success in the first place. Indirect operating leverage, on the other hand, is the result of a lack of strategic approach and application once the wheels are already in motion.

Once we have identified the drivers that could put leverage on our professional and personal lives, we can learn how to navigate ourselves better and appreciate the importance of developing more powerful skill sets to assist us in the creation of wealth. Wealth creation helps reduce anyone's leverage upon us through achieving our financial independence. In order to do this, we need to identify our skill set, find ways to monetize it, and recycle capital for the purpose of continual improvement.

When it comes to identifying your skill set, start with what you know. Your skills may not be confined to your career. You could very well identify skills based on your locations, relationships, social media use, habits of consumption, and so on. Big business often isn't built directly from big ideas, but rather from simple, well-executed ideas that are constantly refining their purpose and core abilities.

The underlying principle of skill set monetization is the understanding that everything must be valuable to someone. If you can find your ways to monetize your skills to that specific audience, you'll be able to generate wealth instead of merely redistributing it. Try to strike a balance between skills that can be monetized instantaneously and skills with high opportunity costs that will eventually be compensated through long-term success.

FINAL THOUGHTS

In many classical Middle Eastern texts, there exists a principle that people should refrain from accessing knowledge until they've learned the proper etiquette regarding the procurement of that knowledge. Knowledge is an immensely powerful being, and if we wish to tap into it, we need to have clear hearts and a conviction to use that knowledge for the greater good. By birth, many of us are lucky enough to be born into families that allow us to access immense amounts of knowledge. I believe that it is our collective responsibility to utilize that knowledge in a way that will assist in solving humankind's greatest problems, while also empowering those who struggle to make a living.

The world can be a confusing, cruel, and battering place. But those experiences are not unique to any one individual. Just like us, those around us are constantly fighting their own battles. My final piece of advice is to be brave, be kind, and be respectful. Be honest with yourself, and especially with your family. Think about the long-term impacts of your efforts, and fight for a legacy that will change the lives of your loved ones for the better. In the end, they're the ones who matter the most, not us. When we're able to detract the focus from ourselves, motivation and vitality come naturally, and we find that it's all the easier to get up, get started, and get to work on making a difference.

AUTHOR BIO

My name is **Duddy Abdullah**. I started my career in Private Equity and became an associate who designed and executed corporate restructuring and turnaround plans until exiting investments back to Fund level. I was then assigned to the public sector to become Special Staff to Chairman of Indonesian Investment Coordinating Board (BKPM) before joining the Family Office outfit. My sector coverage includes Property, Healthcare and Technology, Media and Telecommunication (TMT). My specialization functions are Corporate Finance, Corporate Restructuring and Turnaround, and Digital Transformation.

I am now a Director of Anarya Holding, a Family Office backed Investment Holding Company that invested in Digital, Healthcare, and Emerging Industries, ranging from Biometrics e-KYC, integrated digital healthcare solutions, into genome sequencing company. Our investment theses revolve around solid market fundamental, high barriers to entry, digital optimization, and accountability. Our specialization is exploiting value from managing black-swan risks in direct investments and could be conservative in most situations to preserve liquidity for special-situation events.

CHAPTER 9

Intelligent and Passionate Leadership

BY ISMAEL HERNÁNDEZ

BREATHE DEEPLY before lifting the laser pistol, tighten your abdomen while aiming at the target, position the diaphragm for a better center of gravity, release 50% of the inspired air, place your eyes on the aiming zone. Hold your breath until after your head drops in the water. Breathe every four strokes for one second, breathe out underwater for three. Tilt the body at 45 degrees at the start, support yourself with the metatarsals, use the arm opposite the leg that takes the first step, and increase the stride's length as soon as possible. Breathe through your nose, breathe out through your mouth. Tense the muscles to compact the body. Squeeze the legs and hips three strides before the obstacle, give the rein slightly when jumping, let the horse's hind legs cross the obstacle, and sit close to the body with elbows. This is how you get to the Olympic Games: taking care of even the smallest detail. I am the Bronze medalist of the Rio 2016 Olympic Games in a very uncommon sport called Modern Pentathlon which includes the events of running, swimming, shooting, fencing and horse-back show-jumping.

I never understood the role and value of some skills on my road to the podium. I didn't stop to think about the value of ambition, the role of being adaptable to unexpected circumstances, or the importance of self-awareness while I was going through the process. I recently reflected on key moments of my career as an athlete and mapped them out against the decisive moments in the lives of my role models and surprisingly, I found overlap. This is by no means an attempt to put myself in the same category as these people, but a reflection on how sometimes we can practice leadership unnoticeably and why it is important to make this practice deliberately.

THE EMAIL

In an email from a Fortune 500 company during the Tokyo 2021 Olympics, the CEO mentioned the following:

> *In Japan right now, athletes from across the globe are showcasing their perseverance, prowess, and strength. For me, closer to home, the accomplishments are on full display in our quarterly earnings reports. In both cases, a few themes are consistent—the desire to win, the competitive drive, and coming together as a team.*

For me, with a very diverse background, such words were an invitation to reflection. I've been fortunate enough to learn many traits through sports even before knowing what they were. For me, it was a game, a school, the perfect teacher that taught me resilience, discipline, and passion; however, the words on that email made me think, "That's true, we develop those skills as athletes." Sports are a lot more than what we see on screen, and as the CEO mentioned, they apply to the corporate world. These three components are one angle of leadership, and the ones that I constantly reflect upon.

Leadership is a tricky concept because it can mean different things to different people in different circumstances. Regardless of how complicated it is to come up with one single definition, I can identify a couple of people who are undeniably great leaders and role models. They share common traits but also unique actions; most importantly, they seem to have a magnetic pull, a mystical aura, that mobilizes people around them toward a common goal. Leadership is rarely about just one person, and, in my experience, it is about bringing other people together along the journey. In my personal definition, great leadership is associated with serving others, driving toward a common goal together. This is how my role models embody some themes of leadership.

So, how do we practice leadership? Let's start from the basics. When I was a younger athlete, I always looked at the Russians and Hungarians as the best pentathletes in the world. They were the countries with the most Olympic and championship medals in the history of the sport. My goal as a young and aspiring sportsman was to learn from the best so that one day, I could become like them. I eventually moved to Hungary where I trained for a couple of seasons, trying to learn as much as I could from my heroes. Bringing that same train of thought into leadership, the best way to start is to identify people with leadership skills that you want to emulate.

THE DESIRE TO WIN: ALLISON LEVINE

What gives leaders the desire to win is that tireless determination of always wanting to be better. The truth is that these dreams are at the end of a very tough path full of breakdowns, complications, and most of the time, failure. The greatest leaders seem to have the ability to think about failure as the opportunity to try again, to be better tomorrow. I often correlate the desire to win with resilience. Living in this very fast-paced and changing age will require acknowledging that there might be times as individuals or a group where things might not go according to the plan or where somebody else might be at the top of the podium. The important part is to learn from these moments and be convinced that tomorrow we can be smarter, be better, and try again.

I was a student at Duke when I heard Allison Levine speak through her experience as the leader of the first all-women expedition to the summit of Mount Everest. While I was in the audience, it was evident that she possessed great qualities as a leader. The two that struck me as the most evident were **ambition** and **humility**.

Allison was a well-known mountain climber before starting this new venture. Regardless of how well known she was, she received some push back on the idea of leading an all-women expedition to the highest mountain on Earth. This is where her leadership skill came in to support her plans. It was her ambition and the way she communicated this passion to the brands that eventually led them to become the sponsorships needed for the endeavor. Passion is a great fuel that creates action; the challenge is to create a focus point on which this energy is going to be released. The passion in this case was directed toward the big ascent. She started the climb during spring 2002, but not everything went as planned. This was the moment when she shared with the audience the second trait of her leadership style, humility.

After weeks of attempting the summit and waiting for the conditions to be perfect, they had one opportunity. Allison and her team went for the summit, but a couple of feet away from the highest point, they had to reassess the situation. The weather was deteriorating quickly, and the worst that could happen would be to get trapped in inclement weather during this last stage. With all the ambition that she had and using her years of knowledge and the experience among her teammates, they made the decision to go back with less than 300 feet to go. Life gave her a second opportunity at Everest, and in 2010 she summited the mountain, completing one of the most daring and daunting physical challenges in the world, the Adventure Grand Slam.

Throughout our life, we will have multiple opportunities to practice both. The important thing about Allison's experience in my eyes was bringing the team along and communicating clearly why they were going back without accomplishing the objective. It's a leadership skill to strive for success; it's also a leadership skill knowing when to walk away. There will be mistakes–situations that we did not contemplate. Sometimes we will need to go back and change the original plan. But let us face our mistakes with responsibility and use all the privileges that life gave us to communicate to the people who have always supported us.

Let us be grateful for every opportunity that life gives us–without doing any merit–to deserve it and learn from it. No matter where we come from, or where we have grown up, our path will be full of obstacles different from those of others; some will have more in their path, some will face more complicated adversities, some will have the fortune to enjoy a less winding trail that is much more passable.

COMPETITIVE DRIVE: CAROL DWECK

The drive comes as a natural outcome of the desire to win: to prove that no record will ever be enough, always wanting to reach for progress and improvement. Because competitions can have binary outcomes, I often relate the competitive drive to a growth mindset. In a competition, you either win or lose. If you lose, you are faced with two options: prepare better for next time or quit. If you win, there will be people doubling their efforts to beat you on the next occasion. Human beings are a competitive species; it's in our genes. In my mind, there is nobody who can better explain these ideas of competitiveness, challenges, and the growth mindset, than Carol Dweck.

Carol is a psychologist and faculty member at Stanford. She is the leading authority in research regarding growth mindset and human motivation. She mentions through her research the difference in focusing too much on what can be achieved *now* compared to what can be achieved *yet*.

Throughout her career, she has been able to test (through multiple experiments) the hypothesis of the psychological benefits of rewarding the process and not the results. It's not that the result is not important. But it is not the most important of it all. The lesson here is that having a solid process, thinking about yet versus now, enables at a psychological level to have more perception of control of our actions. A growth mindset transforms the meaning of effort and an adverse result. In the past, it meant that "you are not good enough," but with a growth mindset, it presumes that a bad result only means that you have a chance to improve tomorrow.

So, is it within our control to foster success? I guess nobody has yet unveiled the formula to success, but I am sure that a growth mindset is one of the tools for creating opportunities out of failures.

By making this subtle change in our mindset from thinking about a fixed outcome when the results are not what we expected, to a more refreshing acknowledgement of "we need to work harder and smarter," we allow for and create growth. The insight is as follows: We have the power to always have that growth mindset on and strive to become the best while competing fairly and with sportsmanship.

In her book, *The New Psychology of Success*, Dweck helps us explore how our conscious and unconscious thoughts affect us and our performance. Dweck postulates how something as simple as the words and narrative we use to communicate with others as well as for ourselves can have a powerful impact on our ability to improve our results.

Whether consciously or unconsciously, Dweck's work shows the power of our beliefs and how they can strongly impact what we desire and whether we succeed in getting it.

In other words, much of what we think we understand of our personality comes from our own 'mindset,' which can both help us and prevent us from fulfilling our greatest potential.

Let's change the narrative. Let's change our words. Let's change our mindset as every result, whether good or bad, will always be an opportunity to be smarter. For me, this is a component of leadership, the ability to reframe misfortune as a new chance to be better.

TEAMWORK: THE GREAT BRITAIN CYCLING TEAM

In sport, there is no greater evidence of the impact that the various pieces of a multidisciplinary team have on an athlete's performance than the Great Britain Olympic team. During the Atlanta '96 games, the British finishing with a single gold medal was considered one of their biggest failures in their sporting history; twenty-five years later they are a sports powerhouse. As a team, they ranked fourth in the Olympic medal table with 65 Olympic medals.

What happened in this quarter of a century? I found an answer in the UK cycling team. In 2003, a cyclist named Dave Brailsford was hired by the Breton cycling team as the new high-performance director. His methodology was continuous improvement. Dave was focused with great determination to improve 1% in hundreds of opportunities at a time, from posture and seat to nutrition and mentality of the athletes. Everything had to be improved by 1%, and it is the sum of these small changes that generates an extraordinary impact. From 2007 to 2017, the British team won 178 world championships and 66 Olympic and Paralympic gold medals.

Dave was obsessed with measuring everything. The measurements created a frame of reference on which they could produce improvements in areas that had never been thought of. From the equipment that transported the bikes to the physical therapists who warmed up the athletes' muscles before the competition, they were all lined up and in perfect sync, worthy of a Swiss watch. The value of having a synchronized and aligned team is that small changes can make a big impact. But for that synchrony to exist, there needs to be someone leading the group.

This is the ability of a great leader: to see how all the pieces of a team fit together to produce something better than the sum of its parts.

Success takes teamwork. We cannot be leaders by ourselves because, as Malcolm Gladwell said, "...not rock stars, not professional athletes, not software millionaires, not even geniuses have ever achieved success on their own." To set out on a path to climb any mountain, takes a lot of confidence and support. Leadership in a team doesn't need to be related to a rank or a position. There have been plenty of examples of people leading from the middle or leading by example. I'm sure that more than one has been asked in an interview or two, "Tell me about a time when you have led without authority."

Inside our organizations, teams break silos, make results achievable, and keep the spark of innovation going. It doesn't matter if you are not in the spotlight or the arena, your contribution makes it possible. After all, the most significant accomplishments are not the ones that we acquire ourselves but the ones we procure for others.

SERVING LEADERSHIP: AJAY BANGA

It was September 19, 2017 when I heard Mastercard's former president and CEO, Ajay Banga speak for the first time. I remember the date because a massive earthquake struck Mexico City, where I'm originally from, leaving hundreds of people injured and reminding us how vulnerable we are to nature.

He was talking about how the company could support the country as Mastercard was supporting different humanitarian activities by that time. He said it was big companies' duty to serve and mobilize people through actions to the people in need and although serving is not always easy, it's needed if we understand the fact that leaders owe themselves to the people who support them.

The next day I applied for a job at Mastercard. I wanted to be part of a company which cared for the community through innovation and that pursued the gigantic task of creating a truly global economy through financial inclusion.

Ajay is a visionary with a great sense of decency. And while both are amazing traits of a leader that clearly helped to shape the company's culture, the most interesting trait was the competitive drive that he had. He was asked to define who was Mastercard's competition, and while some might have answered with the names of any other card networks, Ajay clearly defined the competition as all the other methods of payments that are still predominant in the world. He also made his "north star" the daunting effort of bringing to the digital economy 1 billion people from the more than 2.5 billion people in the world without access to a bank account, loans, insurance, or even emergency funds. For Ajay, it was not about competition in terms of market share, but about growing the pie and most importantly, sharing it by helping bring everyone into the digital economy.

He championed this idea of "doing well by doing good" inside and outside of the company. His words became a mantra and delivered such an impactful message that it's a clear part of the company's culture nowadays. "We can bend the arc of history toward financial inclusion and a world where more people have the opportunity to enjoy what we take for granted, but it takes all of us working together," he used to say.

HOW EVERYTHING CONNECTS

As we have seen, leadership is rarely about one single event. It's more of a discipline and as such, is one that we have either practiced through our lives or that we can make the deliberate effort to practice on a regular basis. Looking back on my career and my decisions, there are some moments where I could see a hint of my idols' skills in my actions.

My journey to Rio 2016 started with an emotional and physical recovery after failing to qualify to the London 2012 Olympics on two separate occasions. First, during 2010 I failed an antidoping test due to an accidental ingestion of clenbuterol, an anabolic that is widely used in Mexico in the cattle industry to speed up the growth of animals. The substance made its way to my system and that ended up in a one-year ban from any local or international competition. Although it was an accident, the outcome was the same. Ashamed and ridiculed by the media outlets, I did the only thing I could have done, put my head down and kept working. The desire and ambition to compete in the Olympics was too strong.

The second time that my team and I failed to qualify for the London 2012 games was at the world championships in Rome. In that competition, I was well positioned to secure one of the spots at the Olympiad; however, at this point not updating my decision based on new information made me pick the wrong horse. The horse stopped in front of the obstacle, and I fell off the horse hitting my face against the rail. This was the equivalent of not walking back after the weather deteriorated at the top of Everest.

Reassessing and planning the path to Rio 2016 started with the gentle challenge of my coaches and my father. All of them believed I could make it, but for that, I needed to be smarter and define new goals. This new season also required that I get over the failure of not qualifying to London; it was not an experience where I was going to be able to have a second chance.

Finally, I needed to work with my team to increase the probabilities of success. By far one of the most inspiring figures in my life has been my father. He was the unofficial general manager of my athletic career. I remember him always saying, "It takes a team to rewrite history." Everything began with him believing in me before I believed in myself. That belief was contagious and eventually it trickled down to everybody on my team. I was the leader; I was more than just the athlete listening to feedback from my coaches on how to run faster or how to become stronger. I was also structuring the strategy and making everybody in the team believe we could achieve it.

Although there are sports that are completed individually, no athlete got there on their own. An athlete's performance is the display of the work made by coaches, healthcare experts, nutritionists, and physiotherapists who are behind every athlete in the Olympics. In team sports, the reliance on the results in the joint effort is crisper. Without teammates, coaches, and people supporting every athlete, the athletes would not be where they are. The plan was millimetric and even the smallest detail was considered. Everything was done in collaboration with my team, each and every one of them providing value from their areas of expertise, and I was the vehicle through which their recommendations were implemented. We changed 1% in multiple things, just like the English cycling team. It takes a team to rewrite history, and we were ready for the competitions.

The outcome of this process was a historical achievement the night of August 20, 2016. Everything started with fencing, a good event with a similar number of victories and defeats. Swimming and horseback riding were meaningful events that I prepared with my team to be flawless. It worked. The climax of the competition came during the last 800 meters of the 3200m laser-run event.

The Italian competitor had bested me in the past. He was well-known for his finishing sprints. For that reason, I knew that I needed to control the competition, or he would best me one more time. I passed Riccardo De Lucca, about 400 meters away from the finish line in the Rio 2016 Olympics. I was in the third position with my legs exhausted, so numb that I could barely continue running. Suddenly, the camera focused on me and straight ahead on top of the camera was a big screen. I realized that life was accidentally giving me a rearview mirror on the screen before me.

On the screen I was able to see the rest of the competitors running at full pace and all the moments that led me to that specific track. I remembered the first Olympic Games I watched on television. It reminded me of all the competitions that I had to win, all the training sessions that made me angry or frustrated, all the parties I did not attend, all the personal relationships that I ended up sacrificing. I saw the failures that pushed me nearly to quitting and all the injuries that I faced.

I saw the Italian (de Lucca), French (Valentin Prades), and Australian (Max Esposito) competitors and their ambitions, too. I saw their breath, trembling as much as mine, their physical fatigue exactly as mine as well.

I heard the voices of my parents and my brother shouting my name in the stands in Rio; the screams of my coaches demanding that I not give up. There were less than 200 meters left. The slowest, fastest seconds of my life.

I realized I was not just running with my legs but using the drive to win as fuel running through my body. The competition was not just about the medal anymore, but a tribute to the people, circumstances, and effort that carried me there. And so, I summoned all the strength left and began to run faster until my body crossed the finish line.

A goal should never stop at a podium. The medal was just a reward; a consequence of hard work, good and bad decisions, team effort, but most importantly, a reminder that leadership is not about personal goals, but collective achievements.

Contrary to sport, leadership is not a race, but a distance and endurance test, a track where we need to push regardless of our tiredness, even though we see the finish line still very far away. Great leaders are driven by passion and discipline. If one wants to become a leader, one must invest time in reaching a goal.

That tireless determination of always wanting to be better is the final ingredient in leadership. Of course, dreams are fuel, fame is nice, social skills are an advantage as well as public relations, a nice voice, or an important name. But real power comes from hard work and determination to act toward a mission, without listening to the devil in your ear whispering doubts or insecurities. The best leaders, as well as the best entrepreneurs, athletes, artists, and businesspeople, were not born being leaders—they were built.

THE NEXT MOUNTAINS

After the competition, I remember seeing the Mexican flag being raised. I was on the podium, and a bronze medal hung from my neck. My objective was already fulfilled, and now what? Uncertainty. As soon as I put my first foot off the podium, I realized I could not stop there.

I had been preparing all my life to climb that podium, but nobody taught me how to step off from it. I dedicated years of planning and training for a medal, but I never trained for the moment after. I went from chasing a dream to not having one the following day.

After 20 years, I needed to find a new dream and reinvent my whole identity. As physically demanding as it was, my routine had become a comfort zone, but now the freedom to do whatever I wanted was more a threat than a reward. It was a challenging stage until I understood that sport had never been the final goal but a series of lessons I needed to learn to become who I am today.

I now know that as my role models showed me, any leader needs to have the ability to adapt to new challenges and reinvent themself. Everybody could be a leader, but only the bold who decide to push ahead of these skills and dig deeper into their flaws will be able to reach new horizons.

I also know that one cannot speak about leadership at a professional level if one is not a leader on a personal level, too. If anybody deeply desires to become a leader in an economic or political sphere, they must be willing to work on becoming a leader in a community sphere as well.

Leadership can be a very complicated topic. Speaking with a couple of friends, I noticed that it's also very overwhelming. It usually comes with a series of questions about whether we are being leaders, bringing people along in the journey, and using our time wisely or not. The refreshing perspective that I got after studying people (and which I aim to emulate in the long run) is that leadership can be obtained and practiced. Leadership reminds me of sports. A skill that needs to be shaped and molded, trained and perfected until the point where we are satisfied with the resulting piece.

We started the journey with identifying people and skills that we wanted to emulate. One leadership style might be different from another. This is where you need to have a self-assessment on what skill and type of leadership fits your personality. It's not that you cannot change it, but adoption is usually faster if we start from the things that come naturally to us. In sports and in my career afterward, I have always tried to start from places that fit my current skill set and interest and expand into new areas. The growth mindset will help you here to frame things as a 'yet' instead of as a fixed 'now.' Overall, remember you might not be in control of everything that is happening around you, but you control the narrative that you tell yourself.

Finally, practice what you want to improve and be deliberate. The best tool to help you on this stage is a journal. Keep notes on actions that you are deliberately taking every week. Reflect on them at the end of the month and adjust if there is anything that you do not feel comfortable with. You are in control of this stage of learning. As an additional way to keep improving, talk to somebody about what you are trying to achieve, allow them to observe, and then after a determined amount of time, ask for feedback. Receive the feedback as an opportunity to cover potential blind spots and as a friendly challenge on how you can become a better leader. Will Durant, a 20th Century philosopher wrote: "We are what we repeatedly do. Excellence, then, is not an act, but a habit." Make yourself accountable on your leadership path and start the training in the same way you would prepare for a race: with passion and intelligence.

We are all on this journey, but if you do not know where to start, pause, take a deep breath, and reflect on where you are currently standing. You are far from where you were, but not yet what you are going to become.

AUTHOR BIO

Ismael Hernández is a Mexican Olympic Medalist, Duke Alumni, businessperson, and entrepreneur. He currently works for Mastercard and is an op-ed writer at the Mexican journal *El Economista.*

Connect With Ismael: If you have any questions or comments, you can send an email to ismael.hernandez@olympian.org.

REFERENCES

ABRAHAM, J. (2001). *Getting everything you can out of all you've got.* St. Martin's Griffin.

CARSE, J. (2013). *Finite and infinite game.* Free Press.

CHAZELLE, D. (DIRECTOR). (2014). *Whiplash* [Film]. Sony Pictures Classics.

CHRISTENSEN, C., ALLWORTH, J., & DILLION, K. (2012). *How will you measure your life?* Harper Business.

DANZIGER, S., LEVAV, J. & AVNAIM-PESSO, L. (2011). Extraneous factors in judicial decisions. PNAS, 108(17), 6889-6892.

DURANT, W. (1991). *The story of philosophy: The lives and opinions of the world's greatest philosophers.* Pocket Books.

DWECK, C. (2007). *The new psychology of success.* Ballentine Books.

GLADWELL, M. (2008). *Outliers: The story of success.* Little, Brown and Company.

KAWAI TSUGUNOSUKE. (2021). In *Wikipedia.* https://en.wikipedia.org/wiki/Kawai_Tsugunosuke

LEADERSHIP. (2021, SEPTEMBER 18). In *Wikipedia.* https://en.wikipedia.org/wiki/Leadership

LOMELI, N. (2021, APRIL 27). *Fact check: No, Albert Einstein did not say famous quote about fish climbing trees*. USAToday. https://www.usatoday.com/story/news/factcheck/2021/04/27/fact-check-einstein-never-said-quote-fish-climbing-trees/7384370002/

MANAGEMENT. (2021, SEPTEMBER 17). In *Wikipedia*. https://en.wikipedia.org/wiki/Management

MAXWELL, J. (2007). *Falling forward: Turning mistakes into stepping stones*. Harper Collins Leadership.

MEHRABIAN, A. (1981). *Silent messages: A wealth of information about non-verbal communication*. kaaj.com. http://www.kaaj.com/psych/smorder.html

MY WIFE AND MY MOTHER-IN-LAW. (2020, OCTOBER 20). In *Wikipedia*. https://en.wikipedia.org/wiki/My_Wife_and_My_Mother-in-Law

SAFAROVA, K. (2020). *The Strategy Journal*. FIRMSconsulting LLC.

SINEK, S. (2009). *Start with why: How great leaders inspire everyone to take action*. Portfolio.

SHARMA, R. (N.D.). *Nothing fails like success*. RobinSharma.com. https://www.robinsharma.com/article/nothing-fails-like-success

TETRIS. (2021). In *Wikipedia*. https://en.wikipedia.org/wiki/Tetris

WILLIAMS, L.E., & BARGH, J.A. (2008). Experiencing physical warmth promotes intrapersonal warmth. *Science*, 322 (5901), 606-607.

ABOUT THE PUBLISHER

FIRMSCONSULTING & STRATEGYTRAINING

At FIRMSconsulting we believe in the power of critical thinking, creativity, and storytelling to teach our clients to solve mankind's toughest problems. Our mission is producing original long-form content to empower a loyal, hardworking, inspiring, well-meaning and ambitious worldwide audience to solve the most important problems and, as a result, make a positive and meaningful impact on the world.

Our clients make a difference because they aspire for more than that which society had intended for them. They do not confuse aspiration for ambition. They choose the latter. They act.

We provide a full range of content development, financing, marketing and distribution services for wholly owned educational programs, documentaries, feature films, and podcasts teaching business strategy, problem-solving, critical thinking, communication, leadership and entrepreneurship streamed in >150 countries 24/7 through feature-rich apps and websites.

At any given time >1,000 unpublished episodes are in post-production. Our digital properties include **FIRMSConsulting.com, StrategyTraining.com**, and **StrategyTV.com**. Our apps include Strategy Training, Strategy TV, Strategy Skills and Bill Matassoni A Memoir.

In addition, we own some of the world's most popular business strategy and case interview podcast channels with >4.5 million downloads and counting, and the world's largest business strategy OTT platforms with >6,000 episodes of original programming distributed on iOS, Android, Roku and Apple TV.

We have financed, packaged or distributed more than 45 premium programs through our wholly owned OTT platforms, including "The Electric Car Start-Up," "The Digital Luxury Atelier," "The Gold Miner," "Competitive Strategy with Kevin P. Coyne," "The Bill Matassoni Show," and we try to focus on social causes like championing the rights of disenfranchised workers.

We take an equity ownership positions in businesses we are documenting to produce programming for our platforms. Such as a gold miner, electric car start-up, luxury brands start-up, and new age cosmetics start-up.

Our programming is analytically and conceptually deep, in that we dig into the numbers and details to help you understand the economics at work, and help you replicate our thinking. "The US Marketing Entry Study" and "The Corporate Strategy & Transformation Study," with

>270 videos each, are programs used worldwide to understand the nuances of restructuring a retail bank and turning around a troubled power utility.

In the scripted space, we create original content combining education with entertainment to deliver business teachings.

Our publishing arm releases original books on strategy, business and critical thinking, such as "Marketing Saves the World" by Bill Matassoni, McKinsey's former senior partner and world-wide head of marketing and "Succeeding as a Management Consultant."

We teach business and critical thinking skills to children and young adults, with original and entertaining novels and programming merging entertainment and business training. We believe children and young adults will have a formidable advantage in life if they start learning to think like a strategy partner early in life. STEM skills should be complemented with critical reasoning skills. It should be strategy, science, technology, engineering and mathematics.

We invest in and have exposure to the world's fastest growing market segments and market geographies, including the BRICS. Our subscribers include senior government officials, and leaders of industry and consulting firms, all the way to the executive committee members of the world's leading consulting firms.

We work with eminent leaders such as ex-McKinsey, BCG et al. partners who plan, produce and/or host all our programming. The type of content we produce does not exist anywhere else in the world and is hosted exclusively on our platforms.

RECEIVE ACCESS TO EPISODES FROM OUR TRAINING PROGRAMS:

firmsconsulting.com/promo

GENERAL INQUIRIES:

support@firmsconsulting.com

SUGGEST A GUEST FOR OUR PODCAST CHANNELS:

team@firmsconsulting.com